D1008639

NO LONGER PROPERTY OF
SEATTLE PUBLIC LIBRARY

DEC 0 4 2012

Courage

Courage

Overcoming Fear and
Igniting Self-Confidence

Debbie Ford

HarperOne
An Imprint of HarperCollinsPublishers

HarperOne

Throughout this book, I have used stories and examples designed to help the reader better understand the process. The stories are composites and some names have been changed to protect identities and to ensure confidentiality.

COURAGE: *Overcoming Fear and Igniting Self-Confidence.* Copyright © 2012 by Debbie Ford. All rights reserved. Printed in the United States of America. No part of this book may be used or reproduced in any manner whatsoever without written permission except in the case of brief quotations embodied in critical articles and reviews. For information address HarperCollins Publishers, 10 East 53rd Street, New York, NY 10022.

HarperCollins books may be purchased for educational, business, or sales promotional use. For information please write: Special Markets Department, HarperCollins Publishers, 10 East 53rd Street, New York, NY 10022.

HarperCollins website: http://www.harpercollins.com

HarperCollins®, ■®, and HarperOne™ are
trademarks of HarperCollins Publishers.

FIRST EDITION

Designed by Level C

Library of Congress Cataloging-in-Publication Data
Ford, Debbie.
Courage : overcoming fear and igniting self-confidence / Debbie Ford. — First edition.
p. cm.
ISBN 978–0–06–206892–7
1. Self-confidence. 2. Self-esteem. 3. Fear. 4. Courage. I. Title.
BF575.S39F67   20102
179'.6—dc23   2012002088

12 13 14 15 16   RRD(H)   10 9 8 7 6 5 4 3 2 1

To all the courageous women in the world
and all those who are willing to take the risk
to step into their most courageous self

And to my remarkable sister,
Arielle Ford, whose courage and
confidence has always inspired me

unbound

we may never know
how we hold
all we can
or how the light catches us
when we are out of breath

it's a sign of healing
to be feeling again

the real breakthrough
can only arise
from heartbreak

that which
cures
reminding us
that it's always about beginning
and then beginning again

as the waves crash me
i trust the sand
to polish my edges smooth
dissolving denial
revealing real while
courage and confidence
ignite my core

contraction and expansion
let the light stream in
and the stillness
after so much thrashing about
allows the body to wring
the sorrow out

as freedom floods
shadows may persist
know your undertow
as you alchemize the dark
and remember
that you always have
the strength to choose
how to engage

the clouds unveil the view
when you are ready to climb
now it's time to notice
the miraculous moments
in your life
as they are happening

this
is the making
of me
and we will walk
courageously
into daybreak
from the night
shining our light
together

—Nancy Levin, *author of* Writing for My Life

Contents

Foreword

In this insightful book, my friend and colleague Debbie Ford has detailed a very inspiring and pragmatic blueprint for living a courageous life. As you turn the pages, you will see her unabashed honesty displayed before you in chapter after chapter. Indeed she has covered all the bases. In between the covers of the book you hold in your hand is a thorough delineation of all that you would ever need to begin living in a confident, self-assured manner.

Debbie writes eloquently of her own personal transformation, from having a fear-based approach to handling the affairs of her own life into being an empowered woman of courage. She pulls no punches, holds nothing back, and I was so pleasantly surprised to note that those punches that she now launches are aimed directly at her own formerly panicky self as she is allowing you to be the beneficiary of her former faintheartedness. There is nothing I need add in this introduction to Debbie's book. She thoroughly spells out a plan for living a personally courageous life. As you read and absorb her profound offerings, I can assure you that you will find yourself becoming more and more equipped to deal with all of your life's challenges from a new and stronger position of self-confidence and, yes, courage as well.

I wish to say a few words about Debbie Ford's own application of this concept of courage. As I read this book, I was astonished at how willing Debbie was to throw all caution to the wind. Here in these pages, Debbie has literally let it all hang out. She has displayed a kind of courage that very few writers are willing to embrace, especially writers as well known as Debbie Ford. I have told audiences for decades that if they wish to move beyond ordinary in their lives, they must be willing to change their concepts of themselves. And in order to do so, they must understand fully that their concept of themselves is comprised of everything that they have come to believe is true. Thus, if they are living an ordinary life devoid of feeling that they are living out their own divine purpose, they must realize that their inner truths have landed them at this place called ordinary. In order to elevate your life, you are therefore challenged to change your concept of yourself, and this means changing what you have previously believed to be true.

This requires a kind of courage that few are willing or even able to muster. To say "What I once believed to be a fundamental truth I now see as a misperception on my part" is to literally let go of your own personal history. To change not only your current behaviors but to take on a new set of truths that requires you to admit that those old truths were indeed lies—lies that perpetuated a way of life that almost always led to disaster in one form or another. This act of owning up to the false beliefs of your past and adopting new truths is a true act of courage, especially so for such an accomplished and public person as the author of the book you are about to read. In this profoundly courageous book, Debbie Ford has done just that. She has not only changed her concept of herself and taken on new truths for herself. She has also provided a brilliant blueprint for you to do the same. Her brutal honesty is her courage.

I watched this courage from a very personal vantage point a short while back at the Omega Institute in New York. Both Debbie and I have been handed opportunities to look deep within ourselves, connect to our divine higher selves—the God within us—and take our assigned roles as teachers of spiritual truths to those who read our books and listen to our spoken word. Debbie stayed in a cabin alongside the cabin that Mira, my spiritual partner, and I shared as we met with and received divine healing interventions from the mystical teacher John of God, who was visiting from Brazil. Each day we would stand next to Debbie as she lay in her bed recovering from her spiritual surgery. We both observed her phenomenal courage as her body, ravaged by years of a rare cancer, went through the withdrawals from John of God's divine intercession.

Debbie never complained, always grateful for each moment of life, even though she was in obvious discomfort, willing to be honest and frank about her long battle with this cancer that she had previously kept in the background, afraid of being overcome by people's opinions and projections—but not now. The fears were replaced by love, a new celestial kind of love brought about by the courage to just be herself and to treasure her own magnificence. We stood as one at her bedside and watched as this beautiful woman put into practice what she has written about so piercingly, so comprehensively, here in this book—all summed up in the ancient adage "Fear knocked at the door, love answered, and no one was there."

Take Debbie's sagacious advice. Let go of your old truths that were all illusions. Here is your truth. You have God within you. Live from that place and all will be well. This is courage. I love this book. I love the way it was written. And most of all, I love you, Debbie Ford. You inspire me.

—Wayne Dyer

A Letter to the Reader

On September 24, 2010, I didn't know I was beginning a journey into a hell I could never have imagined. I thought of myself as a strong, courageous woman who had the confidence to take on whatever came my way. I had fought through addiction in my twenties, a heartbreaking divorce in my thirties, and an earth-shattering betrayal in my forties. I believed my fifties and beyond were going to be a breeze. I not only had survived these traumatic experiences but was also privileged to use my own experience to help others thrive.

It began after waiting for days to get cleared by my doctor to fly to Istanbul, Turkey, for a week of vacation before a European speaking tour. But instead of getting the green light from the doc, I got a much different response. My doctor, Dr. Paul Speckart, who always told me I had more courage than sense, feared that I wouldn't make the sensible choice. He told me that if I got on an airplane to go anywhere, they would take me off the plane wherever I landed and send me right to the hospital. I had commitments to meet my friends Leinia and Stephen for a boat trip in the Aegean Sea and then to teach in Copenhagen and Holland. I was distraught that I wouldn't be able to meet my commitments.

Looking back, I should have been alarmed by all the concern in my doctor's eyes, but I wasn't. I believed that I was invincible, that I would be fine and that nobody else understood. I had been at what I thought was a routine doctor's appointment for a case of walking pneumonia, which I believed was no more than a nagging cold. When I was told I needed to be checked into the hospital, I couldn't quite grasp the gravity of the situation. Upset and angry at all the pressure I felt from the doctors and my family members, I begrudgingly let my mother drive me to the hospital. I was checked in for what they said would be a few days.

Within twenty-four hours, I was in an operating room, stunned that they needed to put tubes in me to get four quarts of fluid out of my chest. As I lay in bed after the surgery, I couldn't grasp how this could be happening, how something as simple as a cold was wreaking such havoc on my system. I couldn't explain why the myriad of doctors who came in and out of my room and reviewed my chart looked at me with such grave concern. Why when I was supposed to be getting better did I feel worse? Why was I getting weaker day by day? Was it because of the now unavoidable fact that despite my best efforts to deny, avoid, or repress it, I had cancer?

In 2001, doctors discovered a cantaloupe-size tumor in my abdomen and they removed it. They told me then that the tumor was malignant but that it was "encapsulated," which meant when they took out the tumor, they took out the cancer. So there was nothing to do except get scans every year to make sure the tumor didn't return. I never entertained the notion that the tumor could return or that it could, in fact, be cancer even though they said it to me many times. When I would check boxes on medical forms, I never checked the "Cancer" box. Four and a half years had gone by and I went for another scan. After the scan, my doctor called me and said, "I want you to raise your left arm and feel right under your armpit." He said, "You have a tumor growing there and three more, one in your spleen and two in your abdomen." I couldn't grasp that tumors had returned, and I minimized it to the few people who knew my secret. Even though I minimized that I had cancer, I pursued different healers. My friend Deepak Chopra sent me to a very holy oncologist, Dr. Daniel Vicario, who prayed with me and prescribed medicines that I didn't take and treatment plans that I didn't follow. In my spare time, I flew with Deepak and Dr. David Simon to the Dana-Farber Cancer Institute to talk to other experts about these very strange tumors that no one seemed to know about. When I didn't like what the doctors there had to say or the drugs they recommended, I flew myself to MD Anderson, the other preeminent cancer center, and left there because I had a full head of hair and didn't seem as sick as all the other people since traditional chemotherapies would not work for me.

I knew in my mind that I should be worried and concerned, and that my health should come first, but I could never feel it. I could never really get it. I was always sick as a young child with different ailments. I was known as the little skinny "malink," the ninety-pound weakling, whereas my sister and brother were big, strong, and muscular. I had made a decision some time in my early teens that I wasn't going to be sick again. So except for my family, some very close friends, and coworkers, nobody knew that I had this rare soft tissue sarcoma, Solitary Fibrous Tumor (hemangiopericytoma), because I didn't even acknowledge it. Denial— known as Don't Even kNow I Am Lying—was still in full effect. And as each year passed, I put the condition further and further from my mind.

The doctors told my assistant, Julie, with me now in the hospital, that the fluid in my chest cavity and the tumor on my chest wall that had already eaten through several of my ribs had forced one of my lungs to collapse, which contributed to causing the pneumonia in the first place. Although the fluid they drained from my chest could not be definitively explained, the prevailing theory was that the tumor was weeping fluid into my chest cavity. So although the pneumonia had brought me into the hospital, it was the cancer that was keeping me there. Because my oncologist was too far away to come see me, Dan Bressler, the father of my son, Beau, and a renowned internist, urged me to meet the newest, smartest oncologist on staff—Dr. Marin Xavier. When I met her, I thought Dr. Xavier was bright, positive, deeply concerned, and ready to fight this battle with me. She promised that she was committed to making sure we had a plan of attack for this incurable and rare form of cancer.

Toward the end of my hospital stay, I was visited by a palliative care doctor, a doctor who focuses on relieving and preventing the suffering of patients. This doctor referred to me as a dying patient. He said he was just stopping by to set up hospice care. I looked at him like he was crazy. I had come into the hospital with pneumonia, which I still believed didn't have anything to do with cancer. I looked over at my assistant like "Is this man out of his mind?" He said he knew I was into all this positive thinking but that somebody needed to be straight with me. He wanted to know if I had talked to my son, my beautiful precious Beau, and if he was ready to let go of me. There was no doubt in his mind that I would be gone in a matter of weeks or a month at the longest. As he continued to talk, I suddenly put my hand up. "I am not going to be in this conversation with you. Who are you to tell me how long I have to live? Are you God?" His expression changed to one of consternation as he told me I was in denial. I repeated, "This is not a conversation that interests me." After he left, I asked Julie, who was sitting in the room with me, "Am I going to die?" I was thinking, "Nobody told me!" Then I called my ex-husband and asked him if he thought I was going to die. He said, "We're all dying, Debbie. It's just a matter of when." Then I asked him if he thought I was going to die soon, and he said, "No." When I hung up with him, I had Julie call Dr. Xavier, my new comrade, and I asked her, "Do you think I'm going to die? This guy just told me that I have to go into hospice care and get ready for my death." She said, "Absolutely not."

I am sharing this news because I finally realize that denial is no longer an option. The universe has been trying to get me to take the blinders off and focus on my health, my life.

Still in the hospital, I could barely walk. I was so weak and tired. I was back in the body of my ten-year-old self, except this time I was skinny and saggy. All I could do now was surrender, let go, and listen to Dr. Xavier. The flood of tears kept pouring out.

I couldn't grasp how just a month ago I had been in great shape, even knowing I had four tumors growing inside of me. How quickly things had changed. When I finally got home fifteen days later and twenty pounds lighter, I went into a severe depression. There were moments when I didn't care if I lived or died. I couldn't imagine my son, Beau, having to deal with me being gone. But aside from Beau, I could find no reason to live. It seemed like I had fulfilled my mission to give back to the world, and I had been fortunate, eight books and hundreds of seminars later, to help hundreds of thousands of people.

For months, I lay in bed trying to get my strength back, then trying to walk, trying to find some source of energy, trying to find a will to live. As I lay in bed, the person I knew myself to be was slowly stripped away from me. The things I had cared about, the way I had spent my days, the way I lived my life fell away. I couldn't muster the energy to hold my iPhone. I didn't have the energy to simply talk on the phone. I didn't have the energy to send a text, let alone teach, write, or connect with my friends. What was once so simple, like climbing the stairs to my bedroom, became a challenge. Before, no matter how sick I was, I could muster the strength to lead a workshop. But here, months later, I couldn't work up the energy or care to have the capacity. Even my reflection in the mirror began to change, my body changed. I looked like a junkie off the street. The medicines I took made my skin bruise easily. The texture of my hair changed. My belly became bloated. My face swelled into a round shape called "moonface." That was the hardest part—losing my looks, an outside reflection of my internal collapse. I stopped recognizing myself in the mirror. Things that I once loved became abhorrent to me. I couldn't imagine what I was going to do with my life even if they found a cure for this cancer. I was living in a world of complete solitude and isolation, shutting myself off from most people and keeping my cancer hidden. My body, my mind, and my spirit were all weak. And my will didn't matter anymore.

In this vulnerable and debilitated state, instead of being filled with my usual enthusiasm and excitement for life, I was taken over by fear. The Voice of Fear sounded off in my mind, warning me in the night. It said, "Who needs this? There's nothing to live for. You can't make it through. These medicines are what is making you sick. You're not strong enough. Nothing's going to work for you." The experiences my fellow teachers had shared of tumors miraculously disappearing couldn't—or wouldn't—happen to me.

Finally, I asked my dear friend Cheryl Richardson for support. We decided that she would support me and start sending me affirmations, expecting nothing in return. Every day, she would text me a beautiful affirmation filled with emoticons, encouraging me to think positive thoughts, to list what was good about my life, to choose faith. Day by day, I would change like a chameleon—one day up, one day down, one day in the middle.

Looking back a year and a half later, I see that I believed I was so courageous. I believed I could stand up and fight off anything. But in reality, I was frozen in fear, unable to shake off my noisy internal chatter or my deep feelings of resignation.

The word slowly got out to my business peers. I soon felt their love and kindness, each one offering me much-needed words of wisdom. Despite the love coming my way, I was still dragged down by the voices in my head.

Once my strength returned, I was able to give a lecture at a Hay House I Can Do It! conference. I felt amazing. While there, I ran into Wayne Dyer, who at this point was more of an acquaintance than a friend. But a mutual friend told me to speak to Wayne. So I walked over to him and Wayne looked at me with the most loving, holy eyes. He gave me a warm, caring hug and said, "I want to share some things with you."

Wayne shared with me his experience of being with John of God, a powerful Brazilian medium and healer, and of opening his heart. We decided to go to the Omega Institute together and experience the presence of John of God. It was this powerful weekend where I was touched by Wayne Dyer and this holy healer that began to shift my attitude—looking for the cure, not the cause.

I also realized that my courage was missing. I was no longer fearless. Instead, I was fearful. I had been teaching about confidence, strength, and vision for years, writing about them and training people to make it through difficult times. And here I was stuck in the middle of my own battle without accessing my own truths—truths that I knew so well.

And so it was with the knowledge contained in this book, *Courage*, that I was able to take control, that I was able to see I was doing nothing more than choosing fear, and that there was work for me to do, both internal and external.

There are so many lessons to be learned. There is no doubt that I was running too hard and fast and that because I had so little respect for my health, I overrode all signs and clues that I needed time off. Even when I got those times, I would quickly fill them in with another project and push my own needs farther back and my health deeper into denial. One of the greatest lessons I learned lying in bed for almost a year was to receive love. Having people just love me and bless me and pray for me from all over the world has changed my life. I didn't think anybody could ever cry as much as I did, but the tears were ones of the deep joy of awakening. I could see how shut down I had been.

I learned that I was a people pleaser. I thought I was the opposite. I would stop and help somebody else before I would ever take care of me. I realized that all the things I had preached about all these years were things I needed to hear. As I preach in my first book, "Attend your own lecture." It has been a miraculous process of awakening.

Only my editor, Gideon Weil, would have asked me to write a book on courage before any of this happened. I thought this would be so easy—a subject I knew something about. Little did I know that I would have to find a new kind of confidence and courage to make it through. After turning the book in to him without a word about cancer, Gideon called me and asked if I would be open to talk about my battle with cancer. The book was months away from release and I figured that I would be ready to publicly share about this disease since my denial had finally lifted.

A year and a half later, I can see the holy design of my illness. I can see that having to stay at home and not having the energy to work gave me the opportunity to reflect on what's important to me, what I want to do in my future, who the people are I want to spend my time and my energy with, and what kinds of boundaries I need to draw. Although I've cut myself off from what might have been called my big inner circle, I am now nourished by the few that I keep close. I've learned that I can't burn the candle at both ends. I've achieved one of my deeper goals, which was to be home with my son, Beau, the two years before he went off to college. I've realized every choice matters. Every choice—what I eat, what I say, what I think, whom I trust, and what projects I work on. Even where I live matters. I finally moved after seventeen years and nine houses in a city I didn't like. Accessing my courageous warrior inside has given me the freedom of "No," "No, I can't," "No, I won't." And forgiveness is essential to everyone.

When I trust my intuition, when I tune into the Voice of my Courageous Self, I hear that the most important thing is to take care of myself first, my son second, my family and staff third, and then all else that follows. I will win this battle one day at a time because I choose to. We are all stronger than we can ever imagine being. Every choice matters starting with today. And today, I choose to live.

—*Debbie Ford*

Introduction

How many times have you felt yourself shrink?

How many times have you made yourself small enough to fit into some role that you wanted no part of?

How many times have you kept your mouth shut when you wanted to scream loudly, or handed over your power to someone who didn't have your best interests at heart?

How many times have you succumbed to an impulsive or addictive behavior rather than making a clear-minded choice?

How many times have you told yourself, "I can't. I'm not strong enough. I'm not courageous or confident enough to be all that I desire to be?"

Every day we are confronted with hundreds of choices that either make us feel confident, strong, and worthy, or rob us of the things we desire the most. Paralyzing fears, repressed self-confidence, and untapped courage are the obstacles that prevent us from making powerful choices—choices that are in concert with our best interests and deepest desires. For too many of us, unworthiness permeates most of our decisions in dealing with our finances, our families, our bodies, our weight, or our self-image.

When we lack confidence, we feel unworthy of having what we want, of speaking our truth, of making radical change that would transform the foundation of our future. When we feel weak, helpless, and powerless, we lack the strength to ward off the thoughts of defeat, negativity, and fear that prevent us from living the lives we want. When we relinquish our own power and deny what we are capable of, we succumb to our addictions, our fears, our unhealthy impulses, and the patterning of the past. We act as if and believe that we are indeed weak and insecure.

Of course, this negative cycle may not be happening in all areas of our lives. We may be thriving at work or in our relationships. But for far too many of us, there are areas where we have lost control, where we can't gather enough strength to break through our fears and meet our deepest desires. Every time we make a choice that is based in fear, we are sealing in the belief that we are unworthy, that we are not good enough or not strong enough to be in control of our own lives, our thoughts, our beliefs, our choices—and, most important, our future. Every time we make a choice based in fear, we teach our minds to believe that we are helpless, hopeless, and powerless—three emotional states that leave us feeling like the victim.

What do we need to be confident, to stand in all our strength, and to feel great about ourselves? We need to rebuild our confidence. And we must begin by improving our self-esteem. We need to learn to love all of who we are—our history, our flaws, our mis-givings, our weaknesses, and our fears. And even more than learn-ing to love ourselves, we need to take love on as a cause. We need to become warriors for love. We need to fight for ourselves and stand up for who we are and what we want to become. We need to be warriors instead of victims, fighters instead of followers.

Why a warrior? Because a warrior lives and acts with great strength, integrity, and commitment. A warrior has ignited the courage within. She can face her toughest emotional challenges and break the old patterns. A warrior takes an aggressive stance toward her opponents—which are, so often, the fearful voices of the enemy within.

Why have we, as women, turned away from our aggressive nature? For too long, we have denied a fundamental part of our-selves. We have chosen weakness over strength. We have chosen others instead of ourselves. Why? Because we've come to believe that our aggressive nature is wrong, that it is unacceptable, un-warranted, or unwanted. Maybe in the past it came out in the wrong way, or maybe somebody else's aggressiveness harmed us. We have relinquished the very quality that can give us the cour-age to stand up for ourselves. But this is not the same aggressive-ness that causes people to harm others for sport, nor is it what drives the warrior gone bad to wield a weapon with the intention to dominate and destroy. Instead, this is the aggressiveness of the feminine warrior that is a part of every woman's heart—on fire with the justice of Rosa Parks; armed with the truth of divine love, like Joan of Arc; and capable of sourcing wisdom from the deepest well of her being, like Helen Keller.

We are all born with a part of us that is determined and aggressive—an inner strength that we call upon when we fight for our children and protect our families. This can be the healthiest part of us—the part of us that has us go after something, to be ready for combat, to be ready to win, and to engage in the battles life gives us. There are times when we have to battle with the dark thoughts that are filling our minds—the lies, the misinterpretations, and the shame. There are times when we need the strength to say "Stop." We need the courage to say, "I'm not going to listen to you" or "That's not true." We need the backbone of a warrior for love if we are to be willing to go face-to-face with that which has made us feel weak, impotent, and unable to change.

This is true whether we've been battling a craving because we want sugar to make us feel loved, or fighting the impulse to spend when we need to save. Maybe we need the strength of the warrior to set a boundary, to say, "No more!" or to stop enabling someone we love. Or maybe the warrior is there to save our lives when we need to fight a disease of our own or of someone we love. A warrior's job is to do this. A warrior isn't thinking, "I'd be such a bad person. What will they think of me? I'll be all alone and I won't have any friends if I speak my truth." Or "I just have to lie down and die because I have a disease." A warrior will instead fight to be set free.

Most women have given up their true warrior in exchange for approval, for position, for the illusion of safety. And those who may feel that they have access to their warrior might be mistaken, because most of the time that feeling is coming from a place of fear rather than a place of love, a place of control and manipulation rather than a place of compassion and understanding. The warrior who comes forth from the ego is a warrior of weakness and control—intent on its own power, designed to protect some shattered self-image—rather than a warrior for the greater power of love. A courageous warrior is a spiritual warrior, ready to fight for the Divine in all its expressions.

A courageous warrior looks at each person as a divine being and each experience as a divine experience. She leads with her heart, powerfully determined to bring about the best in everyone and everything. A courageous warrior speaks out even when everyone is whispering for her to stay silent. She knows that she is powerfully sourced by something much greater than herself and that she can release the judgments of others. Self-approval becomes secondary to divine approval. A courageous warrior stands armed and ready for anything that life might throw her way—a divorce, the loss of a job, an addiction, a hurricane, an oil spill, a family illness, a deep loss, or a heartbreak—because she is filled and sourced each day by divine love and the knowledge that challenge is part of her journey. She knows that every day she will have a choice of whether to succumb to fear or to overcome fear with love, faith, and courage. She is brave enough to leave behind those who might hinder her success or diminish her value. She is confident enough to reach out to those who can help her win. A courageous warrior doesn't succumb to the internal demons that would knock her down. Instead she fights for a higher truth—a higher love.

A courageous warrior doesn't look to her past, her patterns, her family history, or her problems to determine whether she can feel good about who she is. She looks inside herself and to the divine power that created her. She is here to gather the strength to fulfill her potential—which means she will have to face controversy. She will have to break through the limitations of her thoughts and her mind that can trick her into believing she is nothing more than a mere flawed mortal. She will have to be willing to face conflicts that will serve to ignite her strength as she stays focused on her vision of the future rather than on the past. A courageous warrior is a woman who bravely battles with the universal enemy—self-ignorance.

So how does a courageous warrior live? She sees her fears clearly and embraces them with honesty and courage.

When you are a warrior for your flaws, you search out the beauty in them. You make them important. You find kindness and compassion for the very things that make you different. A warrior is able to see the beauty and perfection in every aspect of herself.

When you are a warrior for your body, you search out every good thing there is to fill it with—every nutrient, every vitamin, every thought, every belief. You love your body, and you thank your body in the morning and bless it throughout the day.

When you are a warrior for your finances, you make sure that you have enough resources to take care of your family and yourself now and in the future. You feel the courage, strength, and confidence to go out and pursue work that you are inspired by, or to create a business that you dream about. You save enough money and learn enough about your finances to know what you need to take care of yourself in the future.

When you are a warrior for your family, you don't take family matters so personally, because you know you are part of a clan in which everyone has their lessons to learn. A warrior looks to see not how her family has harmed her but how she can make them stronger and how she can be stronger by standing for them.

When you are a warrior for your past, you find the gifts in difficult experiences. You know that these challenges have been opportunities for you to overcome. You know that in letting go of them, you have achieved a great goal. With each challenge, you rise to a new height. You are prepared to combat the agonizing voices in your head that tell you it shouldn't have happened or that you must be stupid or that there is something wrong with you. You ask, "What voice am I listening to? Am I listening to the Voice of Fear, the Voice of Powerlessness, the Voice of Hope-lessness, the Voice of Helplessness, the Voice of Insecurity? Or am I listening to the Voice of Acceptance, the Voice of Power, the Voice of Confidence, the Voice of Courage, the Voice of Strength, the Voice of Forgiveness?" A warrior knows she has the power to choose which voices will guide her.

When you are a warrior for your future, you wake up in the morning with your vision in your awareness. You are clear about your actions and unshakable in your choices. You are focused on what's in front of you instead of what's behind you. You are focused on what you *can* do, not what you didn't do. A warrior is excited and passionate as she creates the future she most desires.

THE LESSONS

In this book, you will learn that what keeps you stuck and feeling weak and hopeless is nothing more than an illusion of the past, nothing more than the fears (real or imagined) that ruminate in your subconscious. You will understand that everything you've come up against is there not to disempower you but to give you an opportunity to be stronger, more courageous, and more in alignment with your higher or true self. You will see that the obstacles you've endured actually give you opportunities to overcome them and to evolve. You will see that when you look at your life, what once appeared to be fear, pain, and hopelessness will become hope, courage, and love. As you become a courageous warrior, you will find yourself standing up straighter. You will feel the confidence to move forward powerfully. You will no longer look at yourself as a flawed, imperfect woman but will instead see yourself as you truly are—a woman with boundless confidence and courage.

With that, a new self-image emerges in which you feel so good about who you are and what you are that you have the power to accomplish anything. You are a foot soldier for truth—and it starts with your own truth: listening to your own impulses, your own wisdom, and the voice of your highest self. You are the keeper of your highest aspirations and the seeker of the divine design of your own sacred life. And in this alignment, you transcend your old self-image and step into courage, strength, and confidence.

The discovery of being a warrior will shift the very being that you are right now and give you the power and strength to take on any challenge, any day of the week. Even in the midst of your daily life, instead of cleverly camouflaging your insecurity with a business suit or sweats, you can adorn yourself with the shimmering gown of self-confidence and the radiant crown of courage that you so deeply deserve.

So in the name of love, courage, and confidence, let's charge ahead!

Transformation
How It Works

For over fifteen years, I've been traveling around the world teaching people how to make peace with their inner world so they can feel confident and secure as they go about wading through the difficult experiences that arise in life. For the most part, those who come to me are high functioning and successful in most areas of their lives, but somewhere they're stuck. They just can't seem to get past whatever obstacles they find on their path. I've discovered that most of the obstacles that rob them of their joy and happiness and keep them from moving forward come from their childhood, passed down through generations, and often are just the hands that life dealt them.

So now, after writing eight books and watching people transform miraculously in short periods of time, I've come to understand that it's not the knowing of our intellectual minds that can move us forward and give us more confidence and courage. Rather, it's the actual process of transformation, of moving from the head to the heart, that changes the way we feel, the way we act, and the way we see and view reality. The process is a journey where we look inside ourselves and reconnect with what's always been there but often hidden—an enormous power that reconnects us with our confidence and our courage. When I feel insecure, I can feel the fluttering in my belly that now serves as a reminder that I'm disconnected from my source of courage and confidence. Often it takes only five minutes for me to close my eyes, examine my feelings, and reconnect to my source. This shift can take anywhere from a few minutes to a few days, depending on the issue.

I promise you that if you're willing to do the work, you will access the kind of confidence and courage you've always dreamed about. You may have this strength in some areas of your life, but the goal is for you to be able to access it in all the areas of your life.

Many of us too often wake up and say something to belittle ourselves, to minimize ourselves, to beat ourselves up. We don't realize the crippling effect this mind-set has on our lives. We don't realize that every negative thought undermines our self-confidence and diminishes our ability to stand tall in the face of life's challenges and our everyday choices.

Let me assure you that the negative thoughts and things you say to yourself are lies. It's okay to be yourself. You're not the only one in the world who feels scared, alone, stupid, or unlovable. You're not the only one who wakes up at times feeling unworthy, not good enough, hopeless, depressed, or stuck. You're not the only one who feels angry, resentful, or pissed off. These are common feelings, and they provide real opportunities to learn how to be a spiritual being.

Courage takes you through a life-changing transformational process. I've seen it work in thousands of lives. This book is not just motivational, although it will motivate you. It's not just inspirational, although it will inspire you. It's not just educational, although you will learn many things from it. It is transformational. At the core, this book will shift how you see yourself, others, and the world.

The transformational process begins when you look beneath the surface of your thoughts, your beliefs, and your choices, exposing the underbelly of your behavior. In the pages ahead, you will discover the why and the how of your fear-based life—not to make it wrong or to judge it, but to explore, understand, and honor it as the reality that has brought you to where you are today. I promise that your life will alter when you see what has been hidden from your conscious view. When you take the time to explore your behavior without self-deception or illusion, you will be able to clean up the past and glimpse the future you long for.

As you move into the ownership phase, you will begin to take responsibility for all that you've been and all that you bring—and don't bring—to the life you are living. You will learn that you can't help but repeat the past when you are always carrying it with you. This allows you to see how you have participated in the realities you are living and understand that it is not possible to live in a circumstance, situation, or reality unless you have given it your consent on some level—consciously or unconsciously. When you realize that there is a part of you that is actively participating in your daily drama, you will start to let your authentic self emerge. It is then that your fears become secondary to your power, strength, and confidence.

In the final phase of the transformation process, you will discover how to fully embrace who you are as a human and divine being. You will stand in a new worldview, one that is based on the whole you rather than a small part of you. It is in this final stage—when you are able to see, feel, and embrace your divine, confident, and courageous self—that you will feel lit up from inside. It is here that you will know yourself as the warrior of love that you were born to be and feel the support of the entire universe at your side. And it is here that you will regain your trust in yourself and in humanity.

When you are able to embrace the whole of who you are, you are able to hold yourself and your history in your hands and in your heart without judgment, fear, or condemnation. Then, without hesitation, doubt, guilt, or gripping fears, you will regard your past and what you know about yourself with divine compassion—a heartfelt, soft, but unshakable reality. You will step into something new not because you've created it or made it happen, but because your inner warrior will have a home inside you where she can shine and from where she can come forth with ease, grace, and joy. It's effortless. You won't have to struggle when you have fully embraced the totality of your nature.

When you embrace instead of reject who you are, when you listen to your true self rather than your ego-driven tyrant, your heart will begin to open to love. When you have committed to being authentically who you were meant to be without shame, guilt, doubt, or any apology, a joy emerges that is rarely seen except in a young child's face. This shift in your inner world will automatically change what you experience in the outer world. As you alter your relationship with your inner world, as you listen closely and have compassion for your most vulnerable self, the lens with which you view the world changes. Seeing things in this new light, you start to treat yourself and others differently. You look at your patterns not with a harsh hand but with a tender heart, and your external world responds with a vision for your future—your happiness and success—that will propel you toward the woman you always wanted to be.

In part 1 of this book, "A New Paradigm," I will give you an overview of fear, confidence, and courage, and how they affect your life—your thoughts, your behavior, and your feelings. You will enter a new paradigm of courage and confidence—what they are, how they work, and why we are all so hungry for more.

In part 2, "Moving from Your Head to Your Heart," I will guide you step-by-step through what I call the codes of the courageous warrior. These codes are designed to reset your inner world, healing old thoughts, beliefs, and behaviors while you begin the exciting and profound journey of becoming a powerful, confident, and courageous warrior of love.

At the conclusion of each code, there will be a transformational process for you to do as well as a courage activator and a confidence builder to strengthen the muscles of courage and confidence within you. Whether you do the process or not, these simple exercises will help you activate your courage, accelerate your confidence, and strengthen your resolve, supporting the re-birth of the warrior within you.

As you approach the final code in this book, you will view the world and your life from an entirely new place. You will become fascinated and awed by the power, courage, and confidence that fill your body with a new kind of strength. Speaking your truth will become a natural expression of your inner warrior. Saying no without guilt when you don't want or feel like doing something will empower you rather than shame you. You will feel different because you have now accessed the truth of who you were meant to be—*yourself!* Your attitude will shift from a fearful or defensive stance to a heart-opening strength that will guide you to make new, powerful choices and behave in ways that surprise you.

Even if you feel you can't do it, the journey in and of itself will alter who you are at the deepest level of your being. I can promise you this because I have taken tens of thousands of people through this transformational process for the past fifteen years. It works when you are ready to put both feet into the warm, beautiful sea of transformational bliss. So take a deep breath, and just give yourself permission to embrace "I am whole." "I am whole and complete with where my life is as of today." Not "I *want* to be whole," but "I *am* whole." "I am whole and complete and I am ready for the next steps."

I honor you for your commitment to courage. You may not have recognized or acknowledged it yet, but today is the perfect day to begin. So breathe in deeply, and claim this courage as yours.

PART I

A New Paradigm

The Culprit

From as far back as I can remember, they used to call me Scaredy Cat. I was known as little scrawny Debbie Ford who hid beneath her mother's dress, ran from anyone who wanted to say hello, and could never fall asleep without the lights on. Always in fear that somebody was going to leap out of the shadows and hurt me, I learned to hide in corners and sneak peeks at what was going on around me. I wasn't more than two years old before I became the neighborhood child who got teased, taunted, and made the brunt of too many stupid pranks. I was vulnerable and scared. I was the youngest of three children and found out early on that no one was going to protect me. The intimidation was happening right in my house, starting with my older sister, whom I idolized, and my brother, whom I believed to be my savior. It was clear by my third birthday that they were bored with my Scaredy Cat act and wished I would grow up and be normal like them.

My father, who believed teasing me was a cute way of interact-
ing with me, would come home after a long day of work, pick up
our white Persian cat (who was named Whitey Ford, after the
famous baseball player), get comfortable in his La-Z-Boy chair,
and then in a sweet voice say, "Come here, my little Scaredy Cat.
Come see Daddy." At the time, I loved the attention, but the cozy
feeling didn't last. What he believed were terms of endearment
got meaner as he moved on from Scaredy Cat to Pigsnose and
Bucky Baboon. Even though I knew how much he loved me, the
teasing hurt, and I became increasingly frightened of the people
around me and the world at large.

As I got older, I learned that scaredy cats weren't widely ac-
cepted. Just like with my brother and sister, I could see that my
guarded and anxious persona wasn't very appealing out in the
world. I wanted to be strong and confident, but instead I was suspi-
cious and fearful. Everything about who I was embarrassed me. I
was awkward and yet wanted nothing more than to fit in and have
the confidence of my older sister, Arielle. With her long, dark hair,
she was the shining star who never seemed to be bothered by anything. I began a search to discover how I could feel that way, too.

Food seemed to change the way I felt inside. By chance, we
happened to live across from a 7-Eleven store on 46th Avenue in
Hollywood, Florida. It was a boring little town to me, and my en-
tertainment became sneaking into my mother's and father's wallets,
grabbing a few dollars, and then racing across the street to score
my fix of Sara Lee brownies and Coca-Cola. This always seemed
to do the trick. The sugar high gave me enough of a buzz to quell
the constant anxiety that swirled around in my young belly, putting

me in a calmer and more peaceful state. After just a few bites of a brownie and a swig of Coke, I felt lovable—and almost invincible. It never took more than five minutes for me to be lifted out of my fear and into a state where I felt stronger and more confident.

My ultimate moment of humiliation happened in seventh grade. I had mustered the courage to go to my first school dance. I still was embarrassed by my scrawny body, my buckteeth (which were now covered in ugly metal braces), and my general lack of popularity. I felt like I had a stamp across my forehead that read: "Loser. Stay away." I hated how I looked, and I worked hard to find ways to camouflage my imperfections. Like so many, I longed to be like all the popular girls. I was so scared of showing up at the dance and being left in a corner that I decided I needed the coolest dress possible. Since we couldn't afford even a semi-cool one, I asked my Aunt Laura to make me a dress. We designed it together. It was burgundy velvet, with a low enough neckline that I could wear a beautiful white ruffled blouse beneath it that would fill in the neckline and give a small trim ruffle around the cuff of the dress sleeve. My hair was long, thick, and beautiful. Now if I could just keep my mouth closed, maybe I could avoid someone calling me Metal Mouth.

Arriving at the dance, I checked out all the other girls and then headed straight to the corner where the "safe" girls were hanging out. They weren't cool or popular, and, without any special status to maintain and protect, they were pretty welcoming. So I found my spot and stayed in the corner, praying that some cute boy would ask me to dance. The music was loud, and the band knew all the latest hits. Things were looking pretty promising.

In a matter of seconds, boys began surrounding me. I was excited. Maybe I had won a prize or was being picked as the best-dressed girl. They were all looking at me with giant smiles, and I felt like I had entered a dream. I didn't have any idea what was going on as they picked me up and started carrying me toward the high stage. Then my heart dropped as I heard the words of Joe Tex's "Skinny Legs and All."

Say man, don't walk ahead of that woman
Like she don't belong to you
Just 'cause hers got them little skinny legs.

You know, that ain't no way to do.
You didn't act like that when you had it home
behind closed doors, alright.

Now you act like you're ashamed at a woman
Or you don't want nobody to know she's yours
But that's alright, just walk on baby.

And don't you worry about a doggone thing at all
Because there's some man, somewhere,
Who'll take you baby, skinny legs and all.

As I fought back the tears, they were holding me half in the air, walking through the crowded dance floor. All I could think of were all the people who could see up my dress. Then, without hesitation, they marched up the stairs to where the band was blaring, "Who's that girl with the skinny legs?" and placed me in the middle of the stage. I heard the entire crowd laughing hysterically at me. The band seemed to love all the laughing and clapping and sang out louder, wanting to capture their glory. Meanwhile, I stood in a pool of tears that I couldn't keep from pouring out of me.

Now, who'll take the woman with the skinny legs?
C'mon somebody please take the lady with the skinny legs.
Now, you all know the lady with the skinny legs

Got to have somebody too, now
Will somebody please take the lady
With the skinny legs, please?

"Hey Joe" "Yeah Bobby?"
"Why don't you take her?" "You-a-fool?
"I don't want no woman with no skinny legs."

On and on it went as I stood in front of my entire school class, shamed and humiliated. I was frozen in fear. All the feelings of worthlessness, not being good enough, and not fitting in filled me. I did everything in my power to fight back the tears and get hold of myself. Even though I wanted to scream and run off the stage, I just stood there, unable to move. Instead of walking away with some confidence and swagger, I stood like a coward, letting myself once again be the brunt of a joke that was anything but funny. Who would want to be my friend? How would I ever find a boyfriend who would want to be with a skinny-legged loser like me? My big night to finally be someone special turned into a nightmare over the course of just one song. It was the worst moment of my youth. I felt branded for life.

I replayed this incident in my head afterward, hoping it would come out with a better ending. But I knew no one would come to save me; no one ever had before. If I was going to survive in this world, I would have to save myself.

My insecurities grew deeper as I devised a plan to just get through the end of my school year. I feared the teasing more than anything else. I remember trying to do anything to be invisible and stay away from the mean kids. Sometimes I even became the teaser so that I wouldn't get teased myself. Every day on my walk home from McNicol Junior High, I cried from a broken heart. All I ever wanted was to fit in and belong. I didn't need to be the most popular girl. I just wanted to be liked and feel safe. But there didn't seem to be any hope of that happening, and without hope my sadness turned into a depression that led me to try to change everything about myself.

Controlled by my fear and my now deeply ingrained insecurities, I made a dramatic decision to turn into the girl that I thought others wanted me to be, not the girl that I was. I began to cover up my authentic, kind nature with a new "I don't give a crap" attitude. And my warm and loving heart quickly grew cold, turning away from feelings of playfulness, affection, and compassion and toward cynicism and belligerence. The pain, humiliation, and fear drove me to become someone other than who I was. I created an outer shell that would protect me and yet separate me from my inner truth. But it was a price I was willing to pay. I no longer would have access to the real me as I became a self-hater who lost the courage to feel her emotions or be seen as she was.

By thirteen, I had started hanging out with the "wrong crowd."

Drugs were becoming popular, and I quickly discovered that they gave me the confidence I was looking for. I had finally found a quick solution for how bad I felt inside. Drugs changed everything, because they gave me a boldness and a bravery that were beyond anything I had ever wished for. I started to learn that being a badass with a nasty mouth kept people from walking all over me. My family couldn't stand the new me, but it was working for the most part, and I even had some friends who liked me. The great cover-up was convincing, and after some time I forgot that this was just a mask I was hiding behind. I worked diligently to find new and better tricks to hide my insecurities—wearing the right clothes (even if they were the cheaper-version knock-offs) and hanging out with the tough girls (even if they were considered bad). It made sense to me: if I could hang with the tough girls, they would protect me from the even meaner girls. But I knew I could never expose my real feelings to them or I would be shunned once again. The petrified little Scaredy Cat still lay beneath the surface of my new, puffed-up persona. I developed a real Tough Cookie act, quickly adding boyfriends and anything else that might make me look cool and hide my pain. I worked on this self-image day and night. But when I was alone, without a belly full of drugs or a boy I believed loved me, I was still filled with a fear that never subsided. But at least it didn't strangle me anymore.

As I grew into a young adult, my awkwardness disappeared. I began taking even greater risks with the help of a few pills, some stylish clothes, and whatever else I could find to give me the courage to go after my dreams. Money became an important commodity, because it allowed me to buy nicer things. I went to work in a clothing store, where I thrived and found that I had a talent for fashion and merchandising, and I loved it. When I was picking out clothes and styling a customer, I felt authentically confident, proud, and strong—three feelings I hardly recognized. Each day was exciting, and I couldn't wait to go home and tell whoever would listen about the great sales I had made and the cool outfits I had put together. I even developed a close friend-ship via telephone with one of the male store managers. Although we hadn't met in person, I somehow felt like we were destined to be together. When we finally did meet, for our first date, it was love at first sight. For months we were together every moment we weren't working. I loved him, my family loved him, and he seemed to be the kindest guy any of us had ever met.

Then at eighteen, with my confidence stronger than it had ever been in my life, I found out that my first love had cheated on me. Shocked and brokenhearted again, I now felt ashamed and wounded instead of strong and secure. All of the confidence I had built up seemed to evaporate. In seconds, my new self-image was shattered, and all of the feelings of humiliation and embarrass-ment from my past returned with a vengeance. Only this time the painful feelings hit even harder, because I believed that I really had turned a corner and found a new course in life. Not surpris-ingly, I used drugs to get through this tough time. And even though my boyfriend wanted us to stay together and said it didn't mean anything, my shame and anger wouldn't allow it. I wasn't going to let him get away with this, even if it meant losing the one I had loved the most.

So I went back to the drawing board, trying to figure out who I would have to be in order to become lovable and find a man who would be loyal forever. I refined my mask, working to become smarter and more successful. But no matter what I did, there was always something that brought me to my knees and made me confront the hurt young girl who didn't have the courage or confidence to be herself. There was always a bad relationship, a disappointing outcome, a snub, or a failure that would lead me to feeling weak and small, even as I was becoming more and more successful in the outer world. Other people's opinions of me continued to be my monitor for success. I spent more time and money trying to look good rather than caring about how I felt inside. The outer world was all that mattered to me. I picked my friends by their level of popularity and importance, and I worked hard to be a woman who exuded confidence.

By my early twenties, I had successfully created an image that would trick even the best investigator. The facade worked well for a few years, until it cracked open once again when I lost control of my drug use and officially became a pretty girl with a bad problem—otherwise known as a drug addict. That's when I knew I would have to get help or die. I checked into my first drug-treatment center. And when that didn't work, I went to another and then another. When I knew I had finally reached my last chance, I let go, and then, as life would have it, I found peace—on the bathroom floor of the West Palm Beach Treatment Center, where I connected with a power greater than myself. For the first time, I went from scared, insecure, lonely, and weak to peaceful, present, and confident.

This connection happened in just a few moments. Without drugs, sugar, a man, or money, I found the courage to fight my disease (meaning the dis-ease in my mind, body, and spirit) and win the internal war that was raging within. On the dirty bathroom floor of my fourth drug-treatment center, I found my power and inner strength, and for the first time in my life I felt free and knew that I had discovered—even though I didn't understand it—the golden key to confidence and courage. When I finally got up off the floor, I knew that all along I had been missing something inside me and that the key was this inner connection that I knew nothing about. This power within me was trying to deliver a message that would change my life forever. I soon realized that fear was the culprit.

THE INFLUENCE OF FEAR

Fear is a very real emotion that can render us powerless. Much of our power is to be found in the choices we make and the actions we take, with every choice either leading us down the same familiar path or propelling us toward a new future. Without warning, fear can take over.

There is so much turmoil in our hearts and in our heads that it is easy to lose sight of what's truly important to us. We are influenced by the myriad events in our lives—both the joyous and grace-filled events and those that blindside us and leave us hurt, angry, sad, or grief ridden. Every day we make choices and are confronted with different possibilities that shape our future. We often treat these choices as if they mean nothing, as if there will be no consequences, or if there are, we will deal with them later—tomorrow, next week, or whenever. But these day-to-day choices either whittle away at our self-esteem and confidence or add to our character, making us feel stronger and more alive. Our ability to cut through fear and to act with courage is determined by whether our choices are made from thoughtfulness and planning or while we are on automatic pilot (a nonthinking or nonfeeling state that drives us to repeat old patterns).

If you grew up without a strong sense of self, you second-guessed yourself constantly. Confused by the internal, doubt-filled chatter, you most likely shrank in the face of adversity, hid when you needed to be seen, and kept your mouth shut when your voice needed to be heard. Fear will have you choose what you believe will keep you safe even when the opposite is true. It will have you believe that you can't do it, you are wrong, the cost is too high, the path ahead too difficult. Fear will tell you, "Don't even think about it. Stay where you are. It's just not the right time to deal with this." But these are the kinds of lies that keep fear in power and you at a standstill. These are the lies that breed mediocrity and guarantee you an unfulfilled life. These are the lies that you must confront if you are going to bypass a predictable future and leap into an unpredictable yet infinitely beautiful future.

With great persuasiveness, fear disguises itself with the Voice of Uncertainty, filling you with worry, doubt, and even dread. With its continuous haranguing, it undermines you with a loop of self-criticism. Its dubious power comes from convincing you to turn away from your highest truth and succumb to the pain of the past. Every time fear wins, you lose. Every time you choose fear, you lose sight of your highest aspirations. You fall prey to being controlled by your history rather than rising to the future that you desire and deserve. Fear screams out, "Don't let go! Don't give up your grudges, your anger, your grief, or your excuses!" Fear taunts you, telling you that you will surely fail. It happily reminds you of all the times you tried and didn't make it to where you wanted to go. Fear is the monotonous monologue that was instilled in you from a very young age, always spouting its warnings: "Be careful. This can't last. You don't deserve it. No one can have it all. Who do you think you are?" Instead of standing up for yourself and shouting back, "I am a powerful, confident, and worthy woman," you succumb to fear, bow your head in shame, and continue on the path you are on, even if you don't like it—and even if it's taking you down.

The more depressing news is that if you don't take up the battle with fear and win, the voice gets louder and louder with each passing year. It gains strength like a tropical storm. Before you know it, fear has the force and power of a hurricane sweeping through your life, destroying all you've worked for and all you've dreamed about.

If you're not clear about how your Voice of Fear talks to you, ask yourself if maybe any of this sounds familiar:

You're too fat.
You're too old.
You're too short.
You're too stupid.
You're too uneducated.

Nobody wants you.
You won't belong.
You'll be rejected.
You're good for nothing.
You'll never amount to anything.
Your time has passed.

Maybe it shouts out:

It's all your fault.
You made the wrong choices.
Your time has come and gone.

Maybe your Voice of Fear is more of a whisper, always telling you:

Watch out!
Be careful!
What are they going to think of you?
You'll be teased, shunned, ashamed, embarrassed.
You'll make a fool of yourself.

Maybe your Voice of Fear is doubt:

But what if it's a mistake?
What if there isn't anyone else for me?
What if I can't get another job?
It's gotta be my fault.
Don't make a move yet—not till you're sure.
There's somebody else better for the job.
I'm never appreciative or grateful—that's why things don't work out
*   for me.*

Maybe it intrudes in your relationships and tells you:

Don't trust!
Don't open your mouth!
Don't ask for what you need!
Don't give too much!
Don't open your heart!
Don't try again!
Don't let go of control!

Maybe the Voice of Fear is one of denial:

One day . . . some day . . .
I'll handle it later.
I am better.
Look at how far I've come.
I've done enough.
If this is all I have, it's okay.

Maybe your Voice of Fear is defensive or blaming:

It's all their fault!
It shouldn't have happened to me.
Why should I have to change?
Why do I have to get over it?
Why should I forgive?
I'll show them!
They did it to me.
The world did it to me.

Maybe your Voice of Fear comes in the form of confusion:

I don't know what to do.
I'm stuck.
I need help.
I'm overwhelmed.
I don't know what I want.

Maybe fear shows up as self-obsession, listening over and over again to why you don't deserve the body you want, the love you want, the health and vitality that you want, the career that you want, or the intimacy that you want.

Or maybe fear appears as the proverbial pity party that takes place when real grief goes undigested and unhealed:

I don't know if I'll ever get over it.
I can't believe this has happened to me.
I don't think anybody really understands what I've gone through.
At the end of the day, no one really cares.

When faced with our fears (which happens several times a day for most of us), we have learned to avoid, deny, or muscle through them. To access our courage, we must uncover, accept, and embrace our fears. And the only way to embrace our fears is to recognize them for what they are. That is, we need to accept them as misperceptions that have been birthed out of experiences from the past or as part of the challenge of growing. Fear is built into our human operating system. It is a useful emotion that can, however, go seriously awry.

You might have noticed that trying to ignore your fears doesn't usually work. Try as you may, in times of stress or heartache they will appear again unless they are embraced. You can eat over your fears, drink, shop, stay busy, do more, complain, gossip, and on and on—all in the pursuit of numbing out and ignoring the barrier that stands between you and your courage. After accepting that you have your particular brand of fears and acknowledging the cost of letting them direct your life, you begin to get some breathing room in which you can observe them more clearly and with greater understanding. You begin to embrace your fears rather than being ruled by them.

You might have heard the adage "What you resist persists." Understanding this statement is the key to embracing your fears. Resisting, judging, and hating your fears only allows them to have a tighter grip. When you ignore, judge, or hide them, you are actually handing over your power to them. The way to reclaim this power is not to vanquish your fears but to open your heart to the wounded part of yourself—your little Scaredy Cat.

I love and nurture this Scaredy Cat part of myself. I don't try to make it go away or be anything other than what it is—a part of me that carries my fear. When I fail to acknowledge and have compassion for my fearful self, I wind up in a downward spiral of negativity. When I acknowledge my fear and stay open to the gifts that it holds, I have access to the confidence and courage that I need to be authentically who I am.

Although suppressed fear is the culprit behind terrible suffering, when fear is embraced it acts as the fuel that propels you into a world of courage and confidence. Befriended fear is a worthy ally urging you to move forward in the areas of your life where you are unfulfilled or emotionally challenged.

Let's look to our sacred wounds, the ones that are clothed in fear. There we will find the key to clearing our minds and reviving our warrior hearts. And we will find ourselves further along the road to meeting the confidence and courage that will transform our lives.

Divine Confidence

From the beginning of time, great women have written to one another about confidence. The author Astrid Alauda wrote:

> I've spent most of my life walking under that hovering cloud, jealousy, whose acid raindrops blurred my vision and burned holes in my heart. Once I learned to use the umbrella of confidence, the skies cleared up for me and the sunshine called joy became my faithful companion.

Confidence seems to be one of those qualities that most of us long to have more of. We believe that this uplifting feeling is the answer to our dreams, that it will allow us to ask for what we want, let us speak up when we are not being heard, and give us the ability to handle whatever the universe sends our way. In short, we believe that it will make life better. This belief is built on a truth: confidence does in fact make life better. Much better. But there is a kind of confidence that goes beyond the definitions we find in dictionaries or at motivational seminars, and we are about to stop the search for this elusive thing and actually claim it.

We tend to use the terms "confidence" and "self-confidence" interchangeably. However, distinguishing their qualities is pivotal to claiming our courage. When we talk about confidence, we're often referring to situations and circumstances "out there." We say things like, "I'm confident that everything will work out for the best. I'm confident that everyone will show up on time. I'm confident that the judicial system will prevail. I'm confident that they will do the right thing." Although coming from a place of personal belief, this kind of confidence always depends on something outside of ourselves.

Self-confidence is a belief in oneself, a belief in one's own strengths and capabilities. Closely tied to our self-esteem, it is a kind of trust in ourselves. What is interesting to note is that very often we display self-confidence in certain areas and not others. We see this all the time: someone who's confident in caring for and raising her children but not in her ability to run a business; someone who's confident in understanding complex technical data but not in her ability to have a one-on-one conversation; or a performer who's confident in standing onstage in front of thousands of people but not in her ability to have a close, intimate partnership.

The truth is, we need both confidence and self-confidence. They are two sides of the same coin. The state of our personal lives and of our world as a whole is asking us to come to under-

stand confidence at a much deeper level, to reacquaint ourselves
with the true confidence that lies at the heart of the matter.

When we begin to explore confidence, we have to distinguish
it from the false confidence of our ego structure. False confidence
is designed to hide our insecurities and trick us into believing
that we are okay. It is the job of the ego to distinguish itself from
others, so we are trained from a young age to believe that we are
individual human beings, separate from everyone and everything
around us. Convinced of the ego's authority through years of
listening to its repetitive internal talk, we buy into the sad belief
that we are not a part of any divine plan. The ego's full-time job
is to maintain this idea of separation through judgment, comparison, and distraction. We judge that we're better than somebody
or worse than somebody, that we're luckier than somebody or
unluckier than someone else, that we're better-looking than that
person or that we're uglier than this one, that we're special, that
we're more important or less important. This litany of comparison
is happening inside our ego.

The ego employs this strategy of distraction to keep us from
questioning, exploring, and possibly stumbling upon a deep insight or, heaven forbid, a deeper truth. The ego is comfortable
staying in its safe zone of aloneness and, like a partner in the worst
kind of codependent relationship, doesn't want us to get emotionally involved with a higher reality. So we can bet it's our ego that is
calling the shots when we're distracted by guilty pleasures, triviali-
ties, fantasies, addictions, and other people's problems.

Inside this paradigm, we shore up our insecurities by comparing and judging. But the problem here is that the ego is a bot-

tomless pit of insecurities. Like the fears that underlie them, the various defense mechanisms of the ego are often accompanied by loud, opinionated, and arrogant voices that sound like this:

If only I ruled the world, it would be a different place.

If only I was in charge.

I know what's best for _____.

If only they had listened to me.

I know better than any of those other stupid people.

The whole world is filled with idiots.

If only we didn't have to work with all these incompetent people, everything would be okay.

I don't need anybody.

The rules don't apply to me. I can do whatever I want.

I'm in a different league.

I'm better than they are.

This is the ego's false bravado masquerading as confidence. We use it as a protective mechanism that keeps our self-image intact, the fabricated self we have come to identify with so completely. This false confidence prevents us from seeing who we really are and from accessing the state of being in which true self-confidence resides. But its effectiveness is guaranteed to be short-lived. This false self-confidence never really does its job of protecting us from our deep insecurities. We can be all dressed up and ready to go, and then someone can walk by and give us one sideways look, and insecurity is back, rearing its ugly little head. The reason our insecurities can grab us without a moment's notice and take our feeling of confidence away is that we never really had true confidence to begin with.

By definition, false confidence works only when it is talking you and everyone else into believing that you have it all together. But false confidence comes with its own form of punishment when it gets pierced by an experience it doesn't want, like being questioned, doubted, or ignored. Then, without hesitation, it turns into its own hell, condemning you for how you have failed at this unwinnable game. This is when you can be certain that your ego is at the helm. Instead of picking you up off the floor of defeat, it tears you down, diminishing any real confidence that you may have had. Instead of having compassion for yourself, you berate yourself, examining your behavior through the lens of perfectionism. Or instead of acknowledging your own accomplishments, you devalue them by comparing yourself with others. If the impact of this game wasn't so devastating, we could simply write it off as the most boringly predictable pattern imaginable. But we can't be glib about it, because it is tragic. Our ego structure would have us stay myopically focused on our own individual lives, playing on an itty-bitty stage where there is room for only one actor—one separate self. But the truth is that nobody is born to an insignificant life. There is not one life that doesn't add tremendous value to the whole.

Somewhere inside of us we know this to be true; we hear the call (however faint it might be) to head in the direction of this bigger life. Built on a bedrock of authenticity, this life asks us to consider what real confidence is. What would we have to know to actually embody true and authentic confidence?

In order to access true confidence, we must lift ourselves out of the fear of the individual ego structure and live in a brave new world, a paradigm of connection with a force greater than ourselves alone. It may not be easy to lift ourselves out of the fear, but it's a choice that we can make. And even more than a choice, it's a transformation. It takes us to a place where we must completely rearrange our thinking.

THE BELLE OF THE BALL

By the time I reached my late twenties, I had learned how to look confident even when I wasn't. I practiced being one of the popular Miami partygoers, and, most important, I felt like I was special. I went to work for the Cricket Club, one of Miami's posh hot nightspots, as the membership director. I wanted this job so badly because I felt that in an instant it would give me the kind of power that would add to my confidence and shine a big, bright light on me. At the time, Miami was known for its private clubs, where people would come in droves to feel good, to feel special, to feel alive. Everyone would get decked out and show up for a long night of drinking, dancing, and partying that would ultimately end in great sex. Now I would be in charge of who would gain entry into one of these exclusive nightclubs and who would have to wait in line for hours. So each night I got dressed up in one of my many disco-era dresses and went off to my important job. I felt like I was someone.

We often had princes, princesses, counts, dukes, and other dignitaries visit our club. They always arrived wearing the most beautiful Italian suits and Parisian dresses, accompanied by an entourage of security and other followers. Now I had the job of meeting them and making sure they had the finest tables and were taken care of like, well, royalty. And because they always spent a fortune at the club, their special treatment was felt by management to be justified. One evening, we were visited by a European count who became very entranced with me. Of course, it raised my self-esteem level twenty points when he asked me to join his group for cocktails and dinner. Since I couldn't really leave my post, I said I would come and sit with them when things slowed down. The Count and his companions were so entertaining, fun, and different from most people I had conversations with that I became fascinated by him and his world.

The next day, I received two dozen beautiful roses along with an invitation to join the Count in Paris for a few "affairs" (the English word they used to mean "parties") as his date. We met for a late lunch that same day. As you might imagine, I wanted to have a romantic fairy-tale adventure, but I also knew that I wasn't ready to jump into bed and have a relationship with this man. My attraction wasn't one of love; it was one of intrigue. So, as we talked through his proposal, I shared my feelings with him, telling him that it sounded like a magnificent trip but that I in no way wanted to go with him if he expected me to sleep with him. I said it in every way I could, because I knew that otherwise it would be a problem for me. I couldn't imagine that a jet-setting man would want to bring a woman on a date from Miami to Paris, first-class, all expenses paid, if there wasn't at least the possibility of some sex between them. The Count assured me that this was the least of his concerns and that he knew plenty of women who would readily agree to have sex with him. The obvious truth of this statement made both of us laugh, which sealed the deal. And with a little hesitation still lurking, I said yes. We talked about the different parties and who would be there, dignitaries from around the world. Since I didn't know who any of these people were, I just kept nodding my head so I would appear more worldly than I actually was at that age.

The Count asked me if I had the proper clothes to wear. I didn't have any idea what would be "proper," but I told him I had clothes like the dress I was wearing the night I met him, which I believed was stunning. He insisted that such clothes wouldn't work for this weekend and said that we'd stop in New York and go shopping before we went on to Paris. I had stepped right into a young woman's fantasy world.

Two weeks later, after just a few phone conversations, I was preparing to travel to New York and go shopping with the Count. The adventure was now beginning. I was picked up at my apartment, whisked away to the Miami airport, and seated in first class on the plane. I didn't know if he was kidding, but he told me all I needed to bring was a toothbrush, that he would get everything else, including the right luggage. I was picked up at the airport in New York in the most gorgeous black town car and taken to the Hotel Pierre, where I was met by a doorman in white gloves. He quickly took me up to the room to meet the man I would now call "my count." (I'm not sure why, because I didn't want him to be "my" count. I wanted him to be my friend.) In the luxury suite, I saw that there was only one king-size bed, and I asked the Count if that was going to be the arrangement. He very kindly promised that he would not roll over to my side of the bed and that he would honor our agreement, which allowed me to exhale. After a wonderful dinner, we went to sleep early because we had only one day in New York for our big shopping spree.

The next day was definitely like something out of the movies. We first stopped at Louis Vuitton to get my new luggage and then continued on to what seemed like every designer store on Fifth Avenue. Eventually, we landed at Yves Saint-Laurent, where he bought me three of the most beautiful gowns, a coat, jewelry, shoes, and purses. If nothing else, I was going to look really good. With each bag and bracelet, my confidence soared and my enchanting dream became increasingly real. I had certainly had people buy me beautiful gifts before, but this was beyond belief. I remember thinking that the coat cost more than my entire wardrobe for the year. And I could see the thrill the Count was having at being able to dress me up and make sure that the woman on his arm would turn heads. When we arrived back at the hotel late that night and dropped exhaustedly into bed, he was a true gentleman.

The next morning, we boarded our nonstop flight from New York's John F. Kennedy Airport to Charles de Gaulle Airport in Paris. By the time we arrived I was ready for a long bath and a good night's sleep, even though it was only the afternoon. The car brought us to the Plaza Athénée Hotel, and as we checked in to the most beautiful suite I had ever seen, I marveled at every detail, from the bedding to the drapes to the antique couches and armoires. We freshened up, had a bite to eat, and partook of a second uneventful night of sleep.

The next day, Friday, was the first big party—a formal ball with an after-party at the famous Régine's nightclub. As I put on one of my new dresses, a metamorphosis was taking place. With each shoe, with each glove, with the sparkling necklace and my stunning coat, I was filled with a kind of confidence I didn't even know existed. I felt like a million dollars and was sure that I looked like that, too. The ball was beautiful—like something I had seen on the big screen while eating popcorn. Women were lavishly dressed in haute couture and priceless jewelry. The Count did indeed seem to know everybody. And when he pronounced my name with his accent, it sounded to my ears as if he were present-ing a famous socialite from the United States.

From the ball, we went on to the after-party and danced into the wee hours of the morning, arriving back at the hotel at around 6:00 A.M. That was Paris in those days. As I got into bed, I real-ized that the Count had moved too close for comfort. I told him kindly that I was very tired and that I needed to go to sleep. I thanked him for making this magical night and this trip possible. As I rolled over, I thought I heard a snort of disgust, but I decided it would be best to just ignore it.

When we awoke later that day, there was definitely tension between us, and I was starting to feel very uncomfortable. My fairy-princess confidence was beginning to erode—or at least my confidence that this man had any intention of keeping his word. Since we had slept most of the day away, all we had time to do was get dressed for our second event. I put on my favorite of the lot of new dresses—a red satin gown with black velvet inlays that was short in the front and long in the back. (I think I finally gave it away when I was in my forties and admitted to myself that I didn't have anywhere to wear it.) If I thought that the night before was picture-perfect, this night far surpassed it. With tensions between us softened by the celebratory atmosphere, I realized that the Count was quite a good dancer.

Again, we partied into the wee hours and got back to the hotel very late—as the clock struck 4:00 A.M. While I was in the bathroom taking off my dress, he knocked on the door, saying that he needed to come in for a second. I wrapped a towel around myself, and as I opened the door, he said in a strong, harsh voice, "I must have you tonight!" As compassionately as I could, I said I wasn't ready to have sex with him, that we had discussed it and that was our arrangement. I wasn't at all ready for his response.

This sophisticated and almost demure man turned into an angry, hostile, raging maniac. He quickly rattled off everything he had done for me and tallied every dollar he had spent. Over and over, he said, "Who do you think you are?" That's all he could think to say. "Who do you think you are? You're a nobody." My shock quickly became terror. What was I going to do? I was in Paris. I didn't know anyone. I couldn't bring myself to sleep with him. If there had been even a remote chance of romance, he had wiped it away in one outburst. In a few seconds, I went from feeling like a powerful, secure, and confident woman to feeling like a petrified, powerless little girl. All the self-confidence that had me walking into these parties as the "It Girl" from America drained from my body. Now I felt like a small little whore from Miami Beach.

As we got into bed, I couldn't imagine how I was going to sleep that night. On the inside, I was rigid with fear—and with good reason. The Count made a second attempt, demanding sex from me, and after he failed again, he went ballistic. He screamed out at me: "I could throw you out this window and nobody would care! Nobody would know!" I silently cried into my pillow and started thinking about my options. I didn't have a lot of money with me, and I had no idea where my plane ticket and my passport were. I lay very still until I was certain he was asleep, trying to muster up the courage to get the hell out of there. I knew I had to sneak out or something bad was going to happen. I could feel it. This was not a man with a conscience, someone who would be embarrassed or shamed. I had now seen his dark side, and I didn't want anything to do with it.

As I lay in bed petrified, I prayed feverishly for help, for safety, even though I didn't know to whom I was praying. I prayed for courage, for strength, and for protection. I was so terrified that he was going to hurt me. Then I found myself remembering parts of a famous quote by Eleanor Roosevelt. Even though the exact words were not there, their meaning circulated in my mind: "You must do the thing you think you cannot do." My fear tried bargaining with me, saying, "He will wake up. It's just one more day. Have sex with him and get it over with." But then I would hear the words again: "You must do the thing you think you cannot do." I didn't think I could leave, so I knew I must.

Sometime around 6:00 A.M., I crept out of bed, opened up one piece of the new luggage, and crammed in the few belongings I'd brought with me, along with my favorite new dress and jacket. He could do what he wanted with the rest. I went in search of my passport, fearful that he had locked it in the safe, which I had no access to. Luckily for me, it was in his attaché case. But the plane tickets were nowhere to be seen. I took a couple of hundred francs from his money clip, not even knowing what the money was worth but clear that I needed enough to get to the airport. And not long after I gathered my things, I found the courage to run out the door. I went as fast as I could through the hotel, knowing that if he realized I was missing he would call downstairs to have me stopped. God knows what would happen. He'd already told me he could throw me out the window with a threatening seriousness I had rarely heard in my life. So the idea that he could accuse me of theft or some other crime wasn't a far stretch of the imagination.

Outside the hotel, with my head held high, I stepped into a cab and asked to be taken to Charles de Gaulle Airport. Because there were no cell phones in those days, I would have to wait until I got to the airport to make my plans. Luckily, I had one credit card and hoped it would be enough to get me home that day. I waited in the airport for almost twenty-four hours until I could take the most affordable flight home. When they finally found a ticket I could afford, I happily went to the back of the plane and awaited my long journey home, which would include four stops. I was humbled but felt stronger than ever before, because—maybe for the first time—I had my dignity and the confidence to stand up for my truth.

This was the day I found a depth of courage I didn't know I

had. I tapped into a deep reservoir in order to make it through a terrible situation. Two years before, being the people pleaser that I was, I probably would have given the Count exactly what he wanted. That's how desperate for love and approval I was. But my courage pulled me out of the hotel bed and sent me tiptoeing around in search of my passport. And even today, when I'm frightened and having a hard time finding my courage, I go back into this experience to remember and access a certain kind of power within me. I may not always be able to see it or feel it, but it's always there.

Divine confidence is a different kind of confidence: it can never be stripped away. It's strange that we go endlessly searching for it—trying to find it through our accomplishments and capabilities—because it doesn't come from being good at something or possessing vast amounts of information or having a big bank account. It can never be found "out there," because it is within you—a part of your sacred DNA. So when you know yourself, when you know at the core of your being that you're here for a greater purpose, divine confidence is present and palpable. And when your cord of connection with the infinite is acknowledged, honored, and nurtured, the fearlessness and faith-filled trust that make up divine confidence run coursing through your veins.

Truth is the key to unlocking the door to divine confidence. This truth is not a concept that you can understand with your mind. It is not something that can be grasped when filtered through the human ego structure. No, it's a truth that is more humble than that, a truth that can be felt only when you get out of your head and into your heart. When you're blind to this truth, you're left to the limited power of your human will, which—as we all can attest—will not come through for you when you most need it.

This truth has been spoken about since the beginning of time. It has been the secret superpower for those who stand tall in the certainty and faith that they have a divine purpose on this planet. Most of our great leaders and sages have come to this truth, rising above the great cover-up of the human ego.

So what is this truth? What will give us access to this profound and all-powerful force? Why are we here? The answer to this question may be the very cornerstone of this book and the pulsing heart of my work. We are here for one reason and one reason only: *to get closer to the divine force that governs the universe, whether you call that force God, Spirit, Love, or Higher Power.*

All experiences, positive and negative, can help us connect with and remember who we are and why we have come to this beautiful and vulnerable planet. All of our challenges are ultimately opportunities for us to reconnect ourselves with our mission here, and they come to us in different ways. For some of us the catalysts for remembering the truth of why we are here will come as personal issues related to family, intimate relationships, health, weight, finances, loss of a job or career, or addictions—whether our own or of someone close to us. Or the catalysts may come on a larger scale—as a tornado, earthquake, tsunami, flood, or war that leaves us homeless. Each of us will have challenges that appear as problems to be solved rather than as opportunities for us to evolve. For the most part, we have been programmed by our families and our culture to view our difficult and painful experiences as bad and unfortunate events—things we simply need to get over. We try to forget them rather than recognizing them as the holy grail for restoring our innate purpose for being alive on this planet.

True confidence—divine confidence—comes from the deep knowing that we are spiritual beings, whole beings, human beings who are mysteriously and magnificently part of the One, and not separate at all. Until we understand that our value is indisputable, that every single one of us matters, that we each have a unique imprint, a distinct gift, an irreplaceable piece of the divine puzzle and a one-of-a-kind way of expressing ourselves, real confidence eludes us. Divine confidence seems painfully scarce when we don't know our higher self. Until we understand and accept our intimate place of belonging in the family of soul and spirit, we won't make the fundamental paradigm shift by which we are willing and able to take ownership and responsibility for ourselves at the deepest level.

The profound understanding that we are both human and divine has the power to revolutionize our lives. From this perspective, it is easy to see that we are all connected, that we matter—that everything we say matters, everything we do matters, and every interaction we have matters. Instead of putting up with petty behaviors from ourselves, we can choose behaviors and perceptions that are of a much higher caliber. We can live in the awareness that we have been blessed with great love. We can live in the knowledge that every struggle in our lives is happening not only to aid us in the evolution of our own soul but to serve others as well.

When we are rooted in divine confidence, the events and circumstances of our lives make perfect sense. I see how this affects my own life. If I am willing, I can use every experience to serve people. I can experience the peace and joy of knowing that I matter and all is well. I can, in this place of deep and abiding confidence, just be and allow my particular expression, contribution, and gifts to flow from a place of authenticity.

I love it when people say to me, "I just want to do what you're doing." They have no idea. If they did have an idea, they'd probably run for the hills and put their head in a hole somewhere. I know that I have been blessed with and have taken on a particular life. There are a million blessings that come with my life, but there are also a million curses. Whether it's been the path of addiction, breakup, or disease, I go through these periods and see them as opportunities for growth rather than seeing myself as a victim of what could look like a bad joke, because I know what I'm doing here.

The truth at the center of divine confidence puts us right in the present—and the present is no place for a victim. When we've made the connection between our humanity and our divinity, the past and the future aren't the objects of so much drama and neurosis. We don't live in the "What if" mind-set of the victim. There is no "Why me?" or "Poor me" or "I can't." There is no "I'm worse" or "I'm better."

When we know that we are here as part of a divine plan, divine confidence directs our every move. When we live in the certainty that the Divine is our partner, waiting to use us as a messenger of hope, love, and service, we choose to contribute rather than hold back. When we decide to allow our lives to be used, we are released from the torture of our individual dramas, flaws, and stories.

To claim your purpose is the great journey of your lifetime. It is the journey that takes you from remembering to knowing, that leads you from your head to your heart. The courageous warrior within you—the one who has fought the gravitational pull of shame, hurt, hopelessness, and despair—is the keeper of your divine confidence. And she will help you to claim your most holy reason for being.

The Courageous
Love Warrior

Courage is a holy gift that exists within you. It's yours when you
are ready to reunite with it. When you awaken to courage, it
becomes an exciting, life-enhancing force that will lift you back
into your power and guide you home to your authentic nature.
The greatest act of courage is to be and to own all of who you
are—without apology, without excuses, without masks to cover
the truth of who you are. True courage comes not just from feeling confident and strong, but from being the honest, authentic
expression of yourself. Think about how audacious it is to really
believe in yourself. It takes a warrior's courage to acknowledge
that your point of view matters, that your truth matters, that your
gifts matter, and that your presence on this earth matters. You
don't have to earn this right; it's yours as part of your birthright.

A warrior's courage is your lifeline to freedom. Can you imagine being so confident that you feel free to just be who you are? Free to be authentic and straight and to show yourself completely in every moment? Free to be vulnerable and free to be bold? Free to expose all aspects of yourself, even the not-so-charming parts? Freedom reigns when you don't have to put on airs or hide your true thoughts, feelings, and beliefs. Freedom reigns when you can speak your gifts out loud and stand up for your greatness and your greatest truth. Freedom reigns when you embrace the courageous warrior that lives inside of you.

A warrior's courage is sourced from faith. It's a powerful force inside of you, an innate impulse that compels you to take risks and face your fears instead of playing it safe inside a smaller self. A warrior's courage allows you to let yourself be seen as raw, vulnerable, and real. A warrior's courage inspires the greatest acts of authenticity. A warrior's courage is the willingness to be radically honest with yourself and others. A warrior's courage listens to the higher voice of her divine self and trusts her instincts. And when in the presence of what's stopping her, a warrior is able to let go of what she believes she knows and take responsibility for her past, willing to go to battle against her fears, regrets, and past mistakes. A warrior's courage is the ultimate freedom, the greatest gift you can allow yourself to experience.

Most of us think about courage as something we do, something we think, or a decision we make. But a warrior's courage is a gift that we receive at birth. It is a level of consciousness that, whether we have experienced it or not, must be held close, developed, and savored. It is a state of being. When you are standing in and *being* courageous, you don't have to "*do*" courage. When you are *doing* courage, you tend to muscle through a situation or decision, which you have probably done before. This muscling through is not the kind of courage that transcends the moment, because it is more often than not sourced from fear, from "I have to" or "I should." Instead, a warrior's courage is poignant, purposeful, and directed toward where change needs to be made. And, as you will see throughout this book, when you experience a warrior's courage, being and standing in the presence of it, you are clear that the rewards for letting it lead you are infinitely greater than the risks. You were born with this courageous warrior inside of you. She is sacred and holy, beautiful and empowered. She is filled with strength, clarity, and confidence, born ready to participate in the world, to face and conquer her fears, and to reunite with all the other powerful, playful warriors out there.

THE TRAGEDY OF THE COURAGEOUS WARRIOR CHILD

The young, courageous warrior wakes up with love in her eyes and compassion in her heart, ready to do her part in the world. She joyfully runs around her room picking out her favorite undergarments, dress, riding boots, and gloves. Then, with grace and awe, she unveils her beloved velvet cape, passed down to her from generations of strong warrior women. Running her hands gently over the worn, soft velvet, she brings it close to her chest, feeling the power and strength imbued in it. Wrapping it over her shoulders, she feels the thrill of the day to come. She steps outside and slides her foot into the stirrup to mount her trusty steed.

As her hair flows in the wind and her horse begins to gallop swiftly, she is on her way to a nearby village that desperately needs her help. Suddenly she sees ahead of her a band of men spread across her path. Her innocent heart worries that there is something wrong, and she wonders whether they need her help. As she slows down, one burly man screams out, "What are you doing here? Where are you going?" The young, courageous warrior proudly replies, "I'm on my way to the next village, where they need my help. My purpose here is to serve." With a smile still on her face, not understanding why these men are blocking her path, she asks them, "Do you need any help?" And with that, she hears their loud retort. "No! No! Go back!" they scream at her. "Go back! You're a young girl. This is not a job for you. This is a man's world and a man's job." She replies, "I know I'm not a man, but I have all the power I need to serve alongside you." Again, they laugh and yell out, "You're not a warrior of any kind. We are here to send you home!" As the blood drains from her face, she feels the urge to fight back. She is boiling with anger, yet aware that these big men could hurt her.

After more taunting, she pulls back the reins and turns to go home. Slowly riding away, she wonders why it's a man's job. She wonders why she can't express herself and serve others. She never before heard the words "This is a man's world." She wonders, "Is this the truth?" As she allows herself to begin to doubt and question her motives, she hears a voice inside her that she can barely recognize. It is nothing like the Voice of Courage that wakes her up each morning saying, "You are an extraordinary gift to the world. There is nothing you can't do. There is no one in the world like you. We need you." Instead, she hears an unfamiliar voice warning her, "It's not safe out here. You'd better be careful. Who do you think you are? You're nothing special. The world doesn't need you." The young warrior, now feeling unstable and unsure of herself, stops near her home, hidden by the trees. She doesn't understand these feelings that are going on inside of her. She closes her eyes to catch a breath, but when she wakes up from her moment of reflection, although she doesn't realize it, she's not the same. She has fallen into a trance.

Instead of remaining mounted on her noble steed, continuing her mission to aid, uplift, and unshackle the hearts of people everywhere, she does as she is told. Instead of offering the world her fullest potential, she believes the story of herself as a helpless, powerless maiden who has to wait endlessly for her prince to arrive, kiss her, take her away to a better place, and save her from a life of drudgery and meaninglessness. In an instant, she changes from a young warrior conquering fear and injustice to a scared child whom nobody can see, who doesn't matter, and whose voice isn't heard. Thus comes about the death of the courageous warrior child.

THE BIRTH OF OUR STORY

Maybe you can remember the death of the courageous warrior child in you. The reality you see now may just be part of a fairy tale that you made up about yourself and then believed.

The story we tell ourselves about ourselves and our lives either empowers or disempowers us; it either opens us to new possibilities or shuts us down. Many of us create fairy tales about our lives that become the stories that limit our access to a better life. At its highest, our story exists to teach us, to help us grow, to allow our souls to evolve. But we make the mistake of allowing our story to define us and dictate the course of our lives. The stories we choose to tell ourselves about ourselves and our lives dictate who we are and what we're capable of. So to reclaim courage, we must look closely at the events that are tucked away in our unconscious. We must revisit the past and bring awareness and closure to it so that we can be released from the stranglehold of insecurity, fear, and regret.

When you were a child, you probably *ran* to try new things, played on monkey bars, picked up unfamiliar objects, climbed trees, watched bugs for hours, or launched spontaneously into song and dance. And then something happened. Most of us have enthusiastically stepped out, hopped onto our proverbial horse, and then, because of something that was said to us, allowed ourselves to get pushed back into the smallness of our fearful human self. We may have responded by becoming a victim, a codependent, or a people pleaser. Or we may have rebelled but at the cost of our uniquely feminine power as we adopted more masculine traits. The power that comes from our intuitive knowing and emotional intelligence was wholly denigrated and dismissed.

However it happens, all of us create a story about our own lives defined by the events we didn't know how to digest. Unfortunately, many of the incidents buried in our story were painful experiences. Our interpretations of these events and experiences create patterns woven through our beliefs, thoughts, feelings, and especially our fears. Although the patterns were created in the past, they don't stay there. Transporting these patterns into the present unconsciously, we create self-imposed limitations and unknowingly make decisions that influence the rest of our lives. The effects of our choices are pervasive and often leave us feeling weak, shameful, and cowardly.

If we've been weak, scared, and stuck, then we continue to see ourselves as weak, scared, and stuck. When we attempt to step out of the confines of the self we believe ourselves to be, especially anything beyond the women's roles that we know (those of our mothers, sisters, aunts, friends, and colleagues), we get stopped in our tracks—confined by the limitations that have arisen from our very own story. Scared, wounded, and often traumatized in our earlier lives, we go into hiding, wrapping ourselves in a false self-image for protection. Created in the spook house of our unresolved past, this false self is perfectly at home being defined in simplistic and narrow terms. The old self-image, with its outdated operating manual, continues to get churned out by our subconscious mind and continuously projected onto the outer world. It is only when we wake up inside the shell of the image we have created and find the willingness to step outside of it that a warrior's courage floods into our lives and we are able to make conscious choices that will further our highest vision for a powerful life.

Amy, a forty-three-year-old executive, came to one of my workshops battling boredom and burnout in her corporate job. Amy had thrived in her career as an administrator in a high-tech firm. Although she had successfully ascended through the ranks of the company, she was concerned that she had lost the passion she once had for her work. Her coworkers told her she was excellent, and she knew that she was masterful at what she did, but when she went home at night she felt bored and empty. She just wasn't fulfilled. Although she fantasized for more than five years about quitting her job, she was never able to make a plan or take any steps toward moving on, always finding an excuse and listening to the Voice of Doubt that said, "I'm not good at anything else"; "I can't make it on my own"; "What will people think of me?" As we confronted the fears that lay beneath the surface and examined her lack of courage in this part of her life, Amy remembered one time sitting at the family dinner table as a child. She remembered her beloved grandfather, whom she greatly respected, talking about women as if they were second-class citizens. She recalled him saying, decisively, "Men are the only successful entrepreneurs. Women should be nurses, secretaries, or at home with their children." Hurt and shocked, she went to bed that night confused and sad.

Although Amy loved her grandfather and didn't want to blame him for planting the seeds of fear and unworthiness, when I asked her to look at the meaning she chose to assign to this incident, Amy went on to tell me that she decided that night that she could never be one of the great women of the world. She buried her dreams. By sixteen, she had become promiscuous—"the town whore," as she described herself. By seventeen, after having an abortion that sealed in the belief that she was worthless and useless, Amy decided she had to cover up her shame with a new self-image. She quickly got back into her studies and applied to the best college in the state. Because she had been so bright, she was admitted, and she quickly excelled. It was only a matter of months before Amy concluded that this new life would hide the shame she felt so deeply.

So here we were, twenty years later, looking at all of Amy's accomplishments, but deep inside she couldn't access the courage she so desperately wanted and needed. Once she recognized that it was something buried deeply from her past that was blocking her from her courageous warrior, Amy made a plan and left her job six months later. She finally let freedom reign.

We are all born with limitations, challenges, fears, and insecurities. But if we believe that any of these things are the *truth* and the only truth of who we are, we will stay trapped in our stories and the patterns that are now deeply ingrained in our subconscious mind and watch hopelessly as they take over our actions and our choices. We can't access our warrior's courage until we remember who we were born to be and why we are here at this time on earth. To get to this place of a warrior's courage, we must let go of our human drama. We must give up the stories that have ruled our lives and shatter the self-image we created to affirm our story. We must recognize and admit to the ways we have confirmed our story and colluded with our past. We have to distinguish and then let go of the beliefs that have kept us bound to the past instead of bonded to a greater future that is calling to us. We must be willing to give up any version of the self that limits us so that we can become the strong, powerful, courageous warrior we were born to be.

Life is filled with unlimited possibilities for who we can become. But we can't be our courageous self when we find ourselves fearful or stuck in some area. That's when we find ourselves frustrated, tired, bored, resigned, or unfulfilled.

When Jane showed up at one of my workshops, she was easy to spot. A tall woman with long, unkempt dirty-blond hair, she sat in the back row with her arms folded, trying to hide herself in a public place. When she spoke, she was eloquent, intelligent, and dynamic—nothing like her appearance indicated she would be. When we began to explore this disconnect, Jane originally bragged about not caring about her appearance, not wearing makeup or bras like most women, being free from the shackles of feminine care. But as she boasted of her independence and uniqueness, she blushed in shame. When I asked her to look into her past for experiences that may have set up her self-image, she told me about an experience she had when she was eight years old.

One morning, curious and exploring, she wandered into her mother's bathroom while her mother was getting ready for the day. Jane reached out in wonder to touch the powder, the blush, and the lipstick laid out on the counter. Her mother swatted her hand away, saying, "Those aren't for you." While her mother carefully applied her lipstick in the mirror, she looked down at Jane and said, "You're so lucky. Most women have to try. But you don't have to. There's no hope that you'll be beautiful, so you're off the hook, unlike the rest of us." Tears stung her eyes as Jane left the bathroom and went back to her bedroom to read. At the time Jane was too young to understand the hurt she felt inside.

Jane buried her mother's message deep in her subconscious. As she got older and moved into adolescence, all the other girls started playing with makeup and clothes. But Jane wasn't like other girls. She hardly bathed, and she showed up to school in unwashed, manly clothes. She even forgot to brush her teeth or wash her face every day. She learned to avoid looking at herself in the mirror. Her disheveled appearance attracted teasing and derision from her classmates, so she started to will herself to be invisible, isolating herself socially and escaping into books and the life of the mind. She knew she was different from everyone else. And although she told herself she was lucky not to be like them, that she was free in a way they weren't, she wasn't really convinced. Instead of her differences being her badge of honor, they were really her badge of shame.

Looking back, Jane could see that this one incident and the belief she formed as a result of it molded her self-image and set the patterns in her life. She had given up on herself before she even started, and profound self-neglect ruled her life. She avoided romantic relationships at all costs, and to further isolate herself, as she got older she chose jobs she could do from home. At my urging, Jane decided to allow someone to give her an extreme makeover. With a new haircut, new hair color, waxed eyebrows, some cute clothes, and makeup on her face for the first time in thirty-eight years—all a possibility beyond who she ever thought she could be—she was radically transformed. A whole new reality opened up for her as she found herself walking taller, maintaining eye contact—out in the world engaging with people. Because her outside finally matched her inside, she was free to speak out without embarrassment and contribute to the world on a whole new level. Jane's courageous warrior allowed her to open up this one aspect of her life, which then spread to other areas.

Courage takes risk and, most specifically, the willingness to let go of the oxygen mask of our past and to trust that there will be air to breathe in the here and now. We must risk the journey to a higher ground where there is freedom from the gravitational pull of our stories, the pull that comes from years of trying to prove that the stories we tell ourselves, the ones we've made up, are the truth.

In order to make the best choices, we must make a fundamental and radical shift. Rather than relating to courage as a resource that we tap into from time to time, we need to allow courage to *source* our choices and infuse our lives. The choice is ours to make. When we're standing in courage, we make powerful choices for ourselves. We're no longer standing on the shaky ground of a false self-image and a story from the past that requires that struggle. We tell ourselves the truth about whether our choices make us feel weak, anxious, and insecure, or strong and powerful; whether our choices are coming from fear or faith; whether our choices separate us from the Divine or move us closer. We can observe ourselves and know whether we are coming from our story, our fear, our ego, or whether we are standing in the peaceful power of our courageous warrior.

Our search for courage is always an indicator that we're trying to make the connection and access the unlimited power that lies beneath the surface of our conscious mind. In fact, this isn't a power that can be located in space and time, but it is infinitely real. And this power is in the hands of our inner warrior—the courageous one who is unafraid of failure, setbacks, or the disapproval of others. Rather than continuing to gather new pieces of evidence to support our story—to validate it and convince ourselves that it's okay to spend one more day living it—we must take the higher road. We must give it all up—give up our old self-image and the entire story about who we are and how we have lived—to allow our new story of unstoppable courage to emerge.

In order to access a warrior's courage, we must explore why we are so committed to our story and what we are afraid will happen if we give it up. There are important and specific answers that need to be acknowledged and understood. Most of us already know about the hurt we carry. We are familiar with the armor we wear to protect ourselves. We know we are blocked in certain areas of our lives. But we need to go all the way and confront our insecurities, fears, and regrets in order to break free from the ghosts of the past. The fantastic news is that once we do this, we will discover the endless well of courage that has always been there, nourishing and feeding the ground of our lives. These messages will deliver us to the doorway marked "Courageous Warrior"—and on the other side of the door is a new self-image, a more enriching story, and a life we can be proud of.

The journey through the pages ahead will enable you to become a messenger for higher love and service, a warrior woman on a great trek to be closer to her spirit. Your vision will expand because you will understand that you're not here to fulfill your human needs only. You're not here to make the outer world happy, although you might choose to contribute to it. You're not here to give up your dreams for another's, although you might choose to share the inspiration and magic of your dreams. And you certainly are not here to spend a lifetime chasing your cravings for love, approval, and attention and then settling for emotional crumbs. You are here to live as your highest expression. You are here to *be* your beautiful, empowered, sacred, holy self without apology, without explanation, without trepidation. Let us see her. And let us all be changed by the power of her divine confidence and courage.

PART II

Moving from Your Head to Your Heart

The Codes of the Courageous Warrior

The Code of Divine Guidance

For the past twenty-five years or so, I believed I was deeply connected to my spiritual self in a profound and holy way. But one overcast morning in a hotel room in San Francisco, I realized that I had refused to listen to what could have been the most important messages of my life. That morning I was leading a class over the telephone, and we were working to strengthen our trust and to know that there is always someone guiding us—a force, a power trying to move us in the direction of our highest life and protect us from taking paths that will ultimately undermine us. I wanted to guide my students through a very important inner dialogue to reclaim their trust and faith. I asked them to close their eyes, take a deep breath, and go inside themselves to find a time when they failed to listen to the brilliance of their inner wisdom, and to look at the consequences and cost of following their will instead of what I called "God's will."

As I always do when I guide an inner dialogue, I closed my eyes as well and went inside to keep the pace perfect and move to the same place I was asking them to go. I asked the question again: "When did you fail to listen to the brilliance of your inner wisdom? And what were the consequences and the cost of following your will instead of God's will?" Unexpectedly, I was drawn into the process inside my own consciousness, and I saw an entire scenario from my own life. I saw how my dream love had become a nightmare of control, lies, and manipulation. I watched inside my consciousness as I saw myself cower beneath my better instincts (my Godly instincts) in situation after situation, turning away from my divine intuition, which was telling me, sometimes almost screaming at me, to run away as fast as possible. I saw that no matter how clear the evidence and my inner knowing were, even when I did find the courage and strength to run away, my partner was able to convince me I was wrong, and I would quickly lose my strength and succumb to his way of thinking. I had done so much work to try to let go of the situation and accept it. I spent months trying to surrender and shake myself of the anger, guilt, and hopelessness that filled my heart and body.

In this moment of silence and reflection, I felt rage fill my body as the ranting in my mind got louder and louder. I was mad, and I wasn't going to get blamed for this fiasco, this trauma, this deceiver's actions. I had already suffered enough. As I grew more and more enraged and shut down to my higher guidance, it was time for me to ask the group, "Are you blaming the Divine, God, spirit—whatever you want to call your divine power—for this situation? Are you mad at the part of you that was trying to help you and hold you accountable for the choices you made?" My own immediate response was "Of course not," but a lower, angrier voice was saying, "Yes, indeed I do." Feeling righteous, my lower self ranted, "Why weren't you there to stop me? Why weren't you there to save me and protect me?" While the group was finding their own answers, I put my phone on mute. The heaving cries came through and shook my body while I sat stunned at what I was feeling and hearing. I began to fight back as I heard a deeper voice saying, "I tried to help you. I sent you many messages through many messengers."

In that instant, I remembered a trip to the park with Bob after we'd been dating for about a month. When Bob stepped away from me for a moment to engage in conversation with someone else, a woman I hold the very highest respect for walked up to me. As if she was divulging a piece of highly classified information, she looked me in the eye sternly and intently and said, in a quiet voice, "Get away from that man. He is a horrible person." I was shocked, because I had never heard Sarah utter a bad word about anyone. My first impulse was to lash out at her. How dare she try to take my joy and my dream love away from me? I wouldn't have it. I went into my "spiritual teacher mode" and quickly asked her if Bob had done anything to hurt her personally. She said no, but that she knew how many he had hurt and how mean and evil he could be. Again, I ignored her words and asked my next defensive question. How could her opinion be based on hearsay? Without even wanting to hear her answer, I went on to say that people tell only one side of the story and that we can and should share only our own experience, and that since I was the queen of the dark side, I knew that everyone has made mistakes and I was certain Bob was not the person she thought him to be. I encouraged her to reconsider her harsh opinion of him. I gave her a quick peck on the cheek, turned away, and went off to find my new man, whom I had just proudly defended. I felt good inside, like a real woman standing up for my man.

Without question, this was one of the first warning alarms that had come to me. And instead of questioning why this honest and warm woman, who had always been an example of impeccable integrity, would warn me about this man I hardly knew, instead of being curious about why she had stepped out of her comfort zone to alert me that I might be headed for danger, I shut down and immediately began making her wrong. I was shocked at the clarity with which I could see the entire event inside my mind after all this time.

The next memory that came into my awareness was a time only a few weeks after the park incident when my assistant Alice called me sounding scared and hesitant as she began telling me about an e-mail I had received on my public e-mail address. She said she hadn't wanted to upset me so she had discussed it with another woman who worked for me and that they decided they had to forward it to me. I waited anxiously for the e-mail to arrive in my private mailbox, wondering what could be so troubling that these two women I loved and trusted were scared to show it to me. When I finally clicked a few minutes later, I found a letter from Bob's last girlfriend, Kim. In the letter, written in great detail, she outlined the events of her relationship and waved one red flag after another, warning me about Bob's "crazy schemes," as she called them, and how she wasn't just worried about my heart but worried about my money.

She seemed sincere, but her letter made no sense to me. I couldn't relate because I didn't feel like I had enough money for anyone to take. Yes, I had a great career and made enough money to live a decent lifestyle, but money for someone to go after? It was absurd. Anyway, it wasn't an issue since Bob had told me he owned a ten-million-dollar company but was a little strapped for cash—a story I wanted to believe. So instead of rereading the letter and giving the content any significance, I focused on my feelings of rage toward Bob. He had three ex-wives that he hated, and now I was finding out about this ex-girlfriend who also harbored horrible feelings toward him. Didn't he know that I had written a book—*Spiritual Divorce*—that helped people heal their relationships with their exes and their past? Didn't he understand that he could not be part of my world if he couldn't take responsibility and heal his past? Did he not care? How could he have so many bad and broken relationships?

Before letting myself cool off, I picked up the phone and dialed his office. With enthusiasm, he said, "Well hello, darling. To what do I owe this middle-of-the-afternoon call?" Without hesitation, I told him about Kim's letter. I asked him to explain why so many people, especially those in his past relationships, harbored so many negative feelings toward him. He immediately got defensive and said that in the past he had made many bad choices when it came to women. He described those women as liars, drug addicts, and gold diggers, although I had failed to see any signs of the money that he was always bragging about. After our conversation, I felt angry and helpless. I had already fallen deeply in love with this man, a man who had charmed me and my family, who had always shown up with a big smile on his face and a great story, and who always had a reasonable explanation or a believable justification for his behavior—although this time the sharpness and specificity of Kim's letter would be hard to dismiss.

Another memory sprang into my awareness. On our third date, when we were going to morning brunch, we waited for an older gentleman to pull out of a parking space. Bob flew into a rage, sticking his head out of the window and yelling at the "old geezer" to get going or he would get in his car and move it himself. When Bob realized that I was sitting there in shock, he looked at me with a puppy-dog expression—that look you see when you catch someone with their hand in the cookie jar. I could see it so vividly. He blurted out to me, "Was that my dark side? Maybe you could help me with that." These words fed right into my need to help people, because I did indeed believe I could help him. At least that's what I told myself at the time. I didn't know I was really making a deal with the devil.

My mind filled up with what I could now see as at least twenty clear warning signs that I should slow down, do a background check, and look with open eyes at where I was headed. In the middle of my flood of memories, I asked my staff to take over because I wanted to deepen my own process. As I began to hear my students share what they had seen in the inner process, one of my favorite teaching stories came to mind.

There was once a man who had a deep faith in God. He was often heard telling his friends that his chaotic life would work itself out because God would take care of him. One day a huge storm caused serious flooding in the town where this man lived. While other members of the community packed their belongings and fled, the man stayed put, believing that God would take care of him. The water began to seep under his doors and through the windows. A fire truck drove by, and rescue workers yelled to the man, "Come on, you can't stay here!"

"No!" he said to them, "God will take care of me!"

Soon the water was waist high, the streets turning to rivers. A coast guard boat came past the man's house. The crew yelled out to him, "Swim out and come on board!"

"No!" the man yelled back, "God will take care of me."

The rain kept pouring down until the man's entire house was flooded. Then a helicopter flew over his house, and the pilot spotted the man praying on his roof. Lowering the ladder, the pilot got on the loudspeaker: "You, down there, grab hold of the ladder and we'll take you to safety!"

Again the man proclaimed his conviction: "God will take care of me."

Finally, the man drowned. At the pearly gates of heaven,

the man had never felt more betrayed. "My God," he said, "I put my faith in you and prayed to you for my rescue. You told me you would always take care of me, yet when I needed you most, you were not there."

"What do you mean?" replied God. "I sent you a fire truck, a boat, and a helicopter. What more did you want?"

I had to take some deep breaths as I realized that this was exactly what had happened to me. In just minutes, I grew somber and quiet instead of angry and blaming. I could see all the ways and times when I had been tossed a rope to grab on to so I wouldn't drown, but I didn't want to know the truth. I wanted the love, attention, humor, and potential future that Bob offered me. I was so deep into my fantasy story of who I wanted him to be that I never looked at who he really was. After ten or so warnings, the pattern was set in place, and I was the one who had turned my back on my faith, on my divine guidance. I had done whatever I could to bring forth my will instead of seeing the signs the universe was giving me. I even had a therapist who told me this was my stuff to work through and that I needed to stay with Bob because it had little to do with him and everything to do with me—a very bad move.

Before long, my connection to my divine intuition had been quieted to a mere whisper that I could no longer even hear. All I could hear was the voice of my wounded ego with all its fear. It assured me that if I listened to the Divine, I would not get the result I was looking for. I wanted a soul mate, a life partner who was smart, talented, and funny and who loved me beyond measure. Even though I hardly knew him, in my mind I very quickly turned Bob into the fictional character I wanted him to be. Deep down I began to see that my will and fear had taken over this situation and that neither God nor anyone else was going to tell me what to do or what to believe. I had what appeared to be the catch of a lifetime, and my need to control the situation overrode any higher vision that God might have held for me.

The Voice of Control minimized all my impulses and feelings. The Voice of Control told me, "Don't give up! You will never find anyone else if you let go of him. You're too different and unique to find love again. You can make this work." Even though my Grandma Ada had assured me after every one of my teen heartbreaks that there was "a lid for every pot no matter what the shape, size, color, or model," I had stopped believing this. After one failed marriage, I had unknowingly shut the door to the possibility that there were many lids to match my pot. And if I was mistaken and there really was a lid for my pot, I would have to be very patient to find mine.

When I was finally willing to see this situation through divine eyes, I was able to hear the Voice of Faith. It reassured me: "It's time to let go and let God. You are a powerful woman who can take care of herself. Everything is as it should be, and all is in divine order. I've got your back. You can trust me now. So, just listen."

This is the promise of the Code of Divine Guidance: "God can do for you what you cannot do for yourself." Can you imagine what your life would be like if you believed this with 100 percent certainty—believed that you were fully supported and loved more than you ever thought possible? Can you imagine what your life would be like if you believed that you were protected and cared for in all the ways you ever dreamed about?

The Code of Divine Guidance calls on us to know and trust that there is something greater than ourselves as individuals. To live this code fully, we must accept that we are both divine and human. Our human, ego-driven nature drives us to try to control things and act as if we were in charge of the universe. Even though all we want is to feel loved and to belong, often we are left isolated and separate from others. These patterns and the beliefs we have adopted cut us off from the safety, freedom, and possibility that come from knowing there is something greater than ourselves at work in our lives.

The Code of Divine Guidance asserts that there is a power, a creative spiritual force, that is beyond our human imagination. I call it "divine" because it can literally change the entire trajectory of our lives and rearrange our thoughts, our feelings, our actions, our choices, and our future. When we trust that our best interest and the evolution of our souls are the Divine's highest priorities, we will feel the spark inside of us, the spark that is always there—driving us, urging us, and nudging us to evolve. There is nothing to fear, because every single thing that is happening is happening to deliver us a lesson, an insight, or a key ingredient to bring us closer to our highest self and support us in the evolution of our souls . . . whether we can see it or not, whether we believe it or not. The experiences that have challenged us are merely opportunities to know ourselves, to learn, to grow, and to step into the highest, wisest parts of ourselves.

So why can't we see everyone and everything as God, as a part of the Divine? It is because we don't see ourselves this way. We don't think that our every breath is God's breath. We think it is our breath. We don't see every cell in our bodies as a divine cell, a part of a great organism that helps us to stay alive and carry out our soul's mission. We don't think that all our thoughts are God's thoughts. We think they are our thoughts. We judge our negative thoughts as bad and wrong if they do not empower us. We can't even distinguish our divine thoughts because we're so busy listening to the negative thoughts inside our own minds. But without these negative thoughts, we would never have the impulse to improve ourselves, to try to be more than we are or to transcend our human nature.

We have to rewire our thinking. We have to break the pattern. We are in denial about so many things in life because we are in denial about our primary relationship—our relationship with the Divine. Denying our divine nature is what keeps us stuck in the negativity and limitations of our human existence. If we are to rewire our thinking, we must start from the beginning. We must find the divinity in every situation, circumstance, and experience. When we look through divine eyes, there is no judgment, no need to be righteous or to make ourselves wrong. We must be reborn right in front of our own eyes. To believe it is to see it, and when we awaken to our true essence, we suddenly have access to a divine self that is infused with power, strength, and courage.

No longer do we have to work so hard or try to be someone we are not, because we find that we are something beyond our imagination. When we are aware of the miracle that we are, we take pleasure in our exhales, trust in the miraculous nature of our bodies, and know that there is something greater than ourselves keeping us alive each day. But as soon as we go to sleep to the miracle that is life, we go to sleep to the miracle of our true divine essence. As soon as we turn our head from the truth of our perfection, we throw ourselves into a cesspool of negative thoughts of individualism.

We've all had at least a fleeting experience of a deep connection with the Divine in a meditation, in a moment of realization, or at a time when we felt blessed by the universe because everything was going our way. We were able to see the beauty and perfection in everything and everybody, and all the little things washed away and failed to bother us. But as quickly as that moment came, it probably left just as fast, and we were pulled back into the battle between our head (our ego) and our heart, living inside the old paradigm that there are good people and there are bad people. And from this limited perspective, we fall back into the ego's fear, which pushes us right back into our minds and separates us from the only thing that can fully give us back all of our power, all of our courage, and all of our confidence.

The Divine is always speaking to us, guiding us. We are the ones who choose whether or not to listen. We may choose not to listen because of our fear, our addictions, our cravings, or old habits that have taken over and wiped out the beautiful voice of the Divine within. But if we listen closely, we will be able to hear the messages we're receiving. We will know when we have the impulse to take a risk and when we feel we should sit still and wait. Our divine intuition can guide us toward what to eat to be healthier or when to leave a relationship that isn't working. No matter how big or small the issue, the Divine can be our guide, and its guidance can come in many forms. It may come as a subtle intuitive knowing or an overt wake-up call, like a fall in the parking lot that warns us to slow down and not rush. It could be an uncomfortable knot in our belly, or a message from a friend. Whatever its form, this divine impulse is with us all the time, trying to get our attention, wanting us to make our choices from the highest place. Either we can hear it or we can resist it. We can trust it or we can ignore it. It is ultimately our choice.

Looking back, I can see so clearly what was keeping me from following my divine guidance. And now I ask you, What is keeping you from following yours? Perhaps you have an agenda, some other plan you're attached to, or an outcome you are committed to achieving, and so you are unwilling to see that your plan might not be right for you. This would make you not want to trust any divine message trying to come to you. Maybe you harbor resentment or anger toward the Divine for the very situations and circumstances in your life where you've been betrayed, hurt, or disappointed. Or you may believe that if there really were this all-powerful force, everything would be perfect in your life and nothing bad would ever happen to you. The bottom line is that you may not trust or believe in the Divine. You may not trust that there's a bigger plan because if you do believe it, you might be wrong. Instead of mistrusting your arrogant ego self, the very part of you that delivered you to the circumstances you are living right now, you mistrust the part of yourself that's been trying to guide, warn, protect, and support you.

In order to live the Code of Divine Guidance, you need to find the willingness to hand all your worries, your struggles, and your troubles over to a power greater than yourself. Instead of gathering evidence to reinforce everything you have known and everything you have believed inside your ego self, you must bring forth conscious awareness, and choose to have faith. Learning how to connect with and trust in your divine self will open you up to levels of magic and healing your ego could never even begin to imagine. The Code of Divine Guidance invites you to embrace your divine nature and call forth the part of you that knows with absolute faith that every relationship, circumstance, and event is part of your unique divine plan.

To ignite your confidence and reclaim your courage, you must step into the highest vision of who you are. The only way to do this is to make the journey back into the arms of the Divine. Within each painful experience lie seeds of wisdom and the opportunity for new beginnings. The ending of a relationship, for example, can feel hurtful and traumatic, yet it is also a potent time for transformation. A failed business can lead you to opening up to a whole new career and an understanding of your bigger purpose. The Code of Divine Guidance assures you that you are connected to a power that will support you fully in the process of stepping into courage and confidence and transforming your life into something new and more fulfilling than you thought possible.

Although you may believe you have a connection with the Divine, there may still be one area of your life where you are stuck, where you can't find courage and confidence, where you can see you are living from your head rather than your heart. You may still believe you can do it all yourself. This false sense of pride will prevent you from seeing your life with clear eyes. Your ego will remain in charge until you step outside your righteous belief that you are simply an independent and separate being. As long as this myth is intact, you keep the door closed to your higher wisdom.

However, when you step into humility, the doorway through which the Divine can walk into your life, you will be able to recognize that you do not and cannot always know what's in your highest and best interest. When you have faith and trust in the Divine, you will discover the confidence that there is good in your present circumstances even though you may not see it at the moment. Faith opens the door to new understandings, new views, and it gives you access to new perspectives. Living the Code of Divine Guidance allows you to open your heart and mind to the possibility that miracles—unexpected positive events, circumstances, or realities that you didn't believe could or would happen—exist in every moment. When you are connected to the Divine, real change can occur.

When you connect with your spiritual self, a whole new world opens up. You can see situations in a new light. You can feel good even in the midst of a crisis. You can access a powerful source of wisdom that is unavailable when you are dealing only with your mind and what you believe to be the truth. So you must open this doorway and believe in yourself—your whole self—like never before. It is time to stand for all of who you are instead of just parts of who you are. You must look to see where you have closed the door—or never even opened it—to the wisest part of yourself.

THE DIVINE GUIDANCE PROCESS

Find a cozy corner where you can comfortably write. Take a few minutes for reflection, and then write down your answers to the following inquiries:

1. **Memorable moments of guidance:** Make a list of the most memorable experiences you have had when you felt connected to a force, an energy, that you sensed was coming from a divine source. It could just have been a moment of complete exhilaration and being present to the perfection of the universe. What happened? What did it feel like? Was it something you heard, saw, or felt?

2. **Learning from the past:** Make a list of the most significant times in your life when you ignored the clarity and brilliance of your inner wisdom. What were the primary events and the specific messages the Divine was sending you that you didn't see or recognize at the time?

3. **The obstacles:** Is there a belief that causes you not to accept any kind of higher power? What distracts you from receiving your divine guidance? Let yourself see what beliefs, behaviors, denial, or cynicism prevents you from heeding the messages you are being sent. Write it out here.

4. **The costs:** Identify the costs and the consequences of following your will and not the will of the Divine. What have you lost or given up by ignoring your deeper guidance? Make a list.

5. **Receiving guidance for a current challenge**: Is there a challenging situation happening in your life right now? Tune in to the still, small voice within—the one that feels real, true, and full of wise love—and write down what it wants to say to you now.

Courage Activator

Buy a journal to record your moments of courage and confidence. Get one that fits in your handbag so you can keep it with you at all times and add to it whenever you need to do so. Make sure to buy one you really like, one that makes you feel good when you pull it out. If you invest in a journal you love, you will invest more in yourself. Every time you do something you feel good about, something that you feel strengthens your courage and confidence, note it in your journal.

Confidence Builder

In your new journal, write on the first page a list of what you love about yourself. Write down at least seven things. Maybe they're things you're good at, natural strengths or skills you developed over time, or qualities you love about yourself. Find one new thing each day to add to your list. (Then, when you feel sad, anxious, or overwhelmed, you can open up your journal, and the first thing you see will be your strengths.)

Courage and Confidence Bonus

Make a list of seven times in your life when you've been coura-geous.

The Code of Surrender

In the Code of Divine Guidance, we begin to cultivate our faith. Now we are ready to move into the Code of Surrender, which allows us to let go of all that we've been. It calls on us to let go of old beliefs and habits, our interpretations, our resentments, our judgments, our projections, our excuses, and our self-image and all that comes with it. The Code of Surrender has us look deeply at what we're holding on to from the past that doesn't allow us to move forward into a new future—the interpretations, beliefs, and decisions from our past that keep us in the repetitive patterns that undermine our courage and our self-confidence. As a teacher, I find that most people don't even realize what they're carrying around with them or how long they've carried it. There are two ways to live life! One is to always be mindful and willing to let go of and surrender your righteous opinions and beliefs. The other, and sometimes complementary, way is to realize that something is holding you down and do the work to let it go.

I'm reminded of a story I once heard about a young princess who was known across the land for her beauty, her poise, and her grace. Her constant warm smile and the sparkle of kindness in her eyes inspired her fellow villagers. Every morning the princess took a swim across a placid lake as many of those who were comforted and uplifted by her gathered near the shore. On one very special morning, the princess stepped into the lake and began to glide across the water with lightness and ease. The villagers watched the princess as if in a dream—until they noticed a change that snapped them to attention. As the princess neared the end of her swim, her bliss and confidence seemed to falter, and her body began to look heavy, weighted, and weak. Her admirers could see that something was wrong. Concerned, one of the older wise women who were sitting on the bank remembered the rock that the princess always wore dangling from her wrist. Although she didn't understand why the princess wore this rock, she hadn't questioned her about it. After all, she was a princess.

The wise woman, in her old, craggy voice, yelled out to the princess, "Drop the rock! Maybe it's the rock that's pulling you down!" The others joined in, shouting in unison, "Drop the rock!" By this time the princess was disappearing under the water for seconds at a time, but each time she was able to kick her way back up to the surface, sputtering for breath as she broke through. However, she was now sinking as much as she was swimming. She could hear the loud cries from the villagers on the shore: "Drop the rock and you will glide again! Drop the rock and you will be free!" As the princess heard their urgent pleas, her attention went to the rock hanging from her wrist, and she noticed the burden of its weight. As her body was pulled down into the water yet again, she remembered her grandfather handing her this rock when she was a young child. He told her she was to carry it to remind her that her duty was to serve the people and protect her kingdom from the enemy across the wall, who would always be looking to harm them. Her grandfather told her, "Never let go of this. With this in your hand, you have the magic to protect your people."

The young princess, gulping for air as she was being pulled down into the water again, looked incredulously at the rock hanging from her wrist. She had worn this rock with great conviction and couldn't believe that it could have anything to do with her struggle today, since she had been swimming with the rock every day since she was five years old. As she struggled for longer periods of time, she could hear the many different voices chanting over and over again, "Let go! Drop the rock. Drop the rock." Between her gasps for breath, she called back to them in a soft, almost inaudible voice, "I can't. It's mine . . ."

The wise woman on the bank watched the princess disappear and heard her faint words ringing in her head: "I can't. It's mine. I can't. It's mine." She wondered what could be so important that the princess would give up her graceful ease, her freedom of movement, and ultimately her life in order to hold on to somebody else's wishes. Even though the princess was known across the land for her good judgment and her strength, there was one thing she wasn't courageous enough to do. She would not let go of what was weighing her down. One more time, the onlookers screamed, *"Drop the rock!"* And the beautiful young princess took her last breath, murmuring, "I can't. It's mine."

There are places in all our lives where we are holding on, where we are trying to exert our will, where we are unwilling to release the burdens of the past. But no matter where they came from or how long we've been carrying them, in order to be free we must drop the rocks that could ultimately kill off our passion, our purpose, and our strength. Without letting go, we struggle through life instead of gliding.

In truth, there could have been a different ending to the princess's story. On the brink of death, the princess surrenders to the pleas of her people. She unravels the bracelet that has held the rock securely in place, letting it fall off and sink to the bottom of the lake. As she floats up and breaks through the surface of the water, her arms open wide, as if to embrace not only her admirers but the world as a whole. Her usual grace and ease are restored as she breathes in the sweetness of the air. Knowing that she has dropped the burden of the past, she resumes her steady strokes to the shore of freedom. Waiting on the shore, her people shout for joy as they run toward the dock to receive her. Puzzled by her near-death experience, the young princess lies down on the sandy shore, grateful that she was able to release the weight of the past. She makes a commitment to herself that she will never again hold on to anything that will keep her from gliding across the waters of life.

What would have allowed the princess to surrender instead of holding on and perishing? Faith—faith that she was being divinely guided. We need this faith to let go, to surrender. Unbound by time and space, the great sages of every tradition invite us into this sanctuary of surrender. Through their poetry and prose, they remind us that we can know in our hearts the deeper truths that our minds too often struggle to reconcile and understand.

It's natural to want to control our lives as we become adults. But be forewarned: when we don't take our medicine—when we don't drink regularly from the healing cup of surrender—the Voice of Resistance will implore us to hold on tighter. It will tell us that in order to get our needs met, we must control and manipulate the outside world. And let me assure you, it is impossible to feel good about ourselves when the fear that we're going to lose control is running us.

LETTING GO

When I started training a group of students to become Integrative Coaches guiding people through transformational processes based on my body of work, I asked them whether they were holding on to anything that could be robbing them of their courage and confidence. I noticed right away that Barbara blushed profusely as her eyes flashed in a "Busted! How did you know?" kind of way. She confessed that she'd been holding on to a secret, and she offered to share it because she was committed to being a courageous warrior.

Barbara told us, in a voice that shook with fear, that twenty years earlier she had been diagnosed with hepatitis C. She admitted that in her late teens and young adulthood she had been a drug addict, scouring the streets of Harlem to score heroin, which she would shoot up with her boyfriend. We were all shocked by Barbara's admission, since to us she looked like a nice, middle-aged woman with a sweet demeanor. Although Barbara had freed herself from her addiction, she was engulfed by the shame and guilt of her past. When she started to suffer daily headaches, muscle and joint pain, and fatigue, she sought out a medical explanation. Because she never had the courage to admit her history of IV drug use, she was misdiagnosed for over twenty years. Then a friend from her old drug days called her to tell her that she had been diagnosed with hepatitis C, and Barbara knew she finally had an explanation for what she had thought was just a prolonged case of hypochondria. Barbara admitted that from that day forward she lived in a state of fear, anxiety, and worry that somehow this information (which only her husband and her doctor knew) would get out. She lied about who she was because she refused to accept the truth, and she had been in denial all these years.

When I asked Barbara to tell me what the Voice of Control, a voice fueled by fear, said about her disease, she let it all out. The voice told her that people would reject her for being a junkie, that she would die early from the disease, and that nobody would ever love her if they knew the truth. Worst of all, fear continuously fueled the devastation she felt at the thought that she might have transmitted the disease to her child.

Then I asked Barbara what would be available to her if she surrendered, if she knew that there was something greater than herself planning an amazing future for her that she couldn't even see. In surrender, Barbara could see that this disease was giving her a huge opportunity to claim her health, her longevity, and her personal growth. She could give herself permission to just take things one step at a time. She could release herself from expecting to figure everything out. And she could honor that she needed to do something in the world that couldn't be done if she didn't have this experience.

As I asked Barbara whether she was going to choose the illusion of control over the gift of surrender, whether she was going to choose the voice that made her feel weak and insecure over the Voice of Surrender, she lit up with possibility, gratitude, and excitement. It was thrilling to watch her courage and confidence return. And as I write this, just three months later, Barbara is pursuing a brand-new, cutting-edge medical treatment, writing about her experience, and publishing a hepatitis C recovery blog. Surrender transformed the source of her greatest shame into a key part of her mission—to support people in freeing themselves from the shame and blame of hepatitis C, reclaiming their power, and finding the gifts in their experience.

Barbara demonstrated that to experience surrender, we must face our lives with laserlike honesty. As the I Ching says, "It is only when you have the courage to face things exactly as they are, without any self-deception or illusion, that a light will develop out of events, by which the path to success may be recognized." To see things exactly as they are, without self-deception or illusion, is easier said than done, because you may be living in a state of denial, a blurred reality that has you look through the excruciatingly limited lens of your history and the stories you have made up about your life and your human limitations. These are the stories that undermine your courage and sap your confidence. You may be living in a fantasy world, wishing and wanting the world to be a particular way, imagining the way things could have been, should have been, or the way you want them to be.

Avoidance—another form of fear—may have you focus on everything but the reality of your life as it is right now, with all the facts and none of the story. You may eat, gossip, blame, party, overwork, or find a hundred other ways to keep your focus on anything other than what wants and needs to be addressed in your life right now. And even though you may want to be strong, courageous, and confident, you may shudder at the thought of making the changes needed in your life—petrified that you won't be able to do it. So you turn your head away and silently slip back into the trance of denial. Why? Because you feel safe in the story you created. You're comfortable with your smaller and more "manageable" view of the world, easily identifiable by all the familiar excuses, rationalizations, judgments, and fears.

In the places in our lives where we are holding on, where we are unwilling to give up, where we are fighting to maintain the illusion of control, we unconsciously, or sometimes consciously, put up an emotional shield to guard ourselves against fear or pain. But this resistance doesn't protect us. Instead, it actually binds us to the past and keeps us mired in the circumstances that we most dislike. Resistance to the truth about our lives denies us the ability to move forward with our lives; what we resist persists.

When thirty-six-year-old Tia came to train with me, she was frustrated, unable to get past what she described as a bad case of writer's block. She'd been trying to build her business as a life coach, but every time she sat down at her computer to write a blog post, to update her website, to set up a public-speaking event, or to send a letter to a magazine, she would freeze up in fear. She literally couldn't remember what she wanted to say. So she would get up from her computer and clean her house, daydream about her amazing future, or pick up another book on business building—feeling momentarily productive as she searched for the key to move to the next level. When I asked Tia what was stopping her from taking the actions she knew she needed to take, she said she just couldn't handle any more criticism, that she couldn't stand being judged. I asked her when she had been criticized and judged before, and Tia told me about her mother.

Tia's mother was mentally disturbed. One day she loved Tia; the next, she hated her. One day she would call Tia her angel, and the next day she would scream that she was the devil. One day she would give Tia hugs, and the next she would slap her across the face. One day her mother appeared healthy, and the next day she was sick. She was a true Jekyll and Hyde, normal in public but deranged behind closed doors. As a child, Tia was bewildered and confused by this behavior, but she soon adapted. She learned to listen to the way her mother woke her up in the morning, to see whether the house was in disarray, to bite her tongue at the dining table, and to escape to the safety of school as soon as she could. She told me about the feeling of sheer terror and dread in her stomach as each school day would come to a close and she would have to go home to her unpredictable monster of a mother.

She told me about the countless times her mother yelled at her, screamed at her, humiliated her, and criticized her.

As Tia's vulnerable, developing psyche struggled to make sense of what was happening around her, the only conclusions she could draw, the only meaning she could assign, were negative. Without realizing what was happening and how it would affect her life, Tia decided there must be something terribly wrong with her to evoke such behavior from her mother. And as a young girl, one thing she knew for sure was that she wasn't safe and no one was coming to save her.

As Tia recounted these experiences, she was filled with rage, resentment, blame, and anger. The issue was clear to me: Tia couldn't move forward in her career while still saddled with the shame and fear that surrounded her relationship with her mother. She had grown up feeling ashamed of her mother. And Tia was not only afraid of her mother's wrath, but also afraid that others would find out about the dark insanity that was a part of every day of her life. The ground of her life was so shaky from the start that having faith in and surrendering to a protective, divine force were inconceivable for Tia. When I suggested that, in order to allow herself to move forward in her career, she would need to let go of the mother she was waiting to have and instead surrender to the mother she'd been given in this lifetime, she said it was the last thing she wanted to hear. She insisted: "It was her job to be a good mother and to get herself help if she was sick. Why did I have to get the mother I did? It's unfair!"

At my urging, Tia began the process of healing her emotional wounds around her relationship with her mother by first accept-

ing that her mother was mentally ill. As she surrendered to that
sobering truth, Tia could begin to see the gifts of having the
mother she did. She could see that she'd learned from her mother
how to sense people's moods and how to anticipate their needs.
Her intuition and empathy had become highly developed. Tia
was also able to see the choices she made, out of fear, to numb
herself, and she understood in a new light why she had worked
so hard to stay invisible and to play small. She had no faith that
anyone else, or anything else, would protect her. As far as she was
concerned, she was on her own.

Confronting the way that fear had influenced her every move,
she could see how she had been trying to avoid the rejection,
embarrassment, and shame that seemed to be her cross to bear.
She could see how her denial of her mother's mental illness had
drained her life force. It drove her to doubt herself, it kept her
stuck in anger and resentment, it stressed her out, and it made
her hide in many areas of her life out of fear of scrutiny and
confrontation. Now Tia could finally admit that she was scared
when people looked too closely. She was afraid that they would
see she was just like her crazy mother. And, most surprising, Tia
was able to identify the ways in which—despite her repeated and
emphatic promise that she would never be like her mother—she
was like her mother. She got postpartum depression after her son
was born and wasn't able to be there for him—just the way her
mother hadn't been there for her. She could see that she can be
moody and strict. She could see that she had taken on the job of
criticizing herself in the very way her mother had criticized her
as a child.

As Tia surrendered, she felt what she described as an unfamiliar feeling toward her mother, one of love. One morning when she went to church and was asked to call out a name of someone she wanted to pray for, immediately Tia thought of her mother—the person she had hated and blamed all her life, and the last person on earth that she would ever think she wanted to pray for. She felt the prayer for her mother passing her lips: "Dear God, please bring my mother release from her pain. Please help her to find peace inside her heart. Please relieve her of the suffering and allow her heart to mend each day in your loving embrace." Tia understood that she could finally let go and step into the new life that had seemed like a distant dream. She could trust that she was growing and evolving right on schedule.

Do you want to struggle to maintain control over what you can't control anyway? Or do you want to surrender your life to its divine design? Do you want to choose resistance and struggle, or do you want to choose surrender, which will restore your confidence and courage, allowing you to move forward? No one can be a warrior for you. No one can make this choice but you.

We have to make the choices and surround ourselves with people who make us feel strong and can see who we are beyond the limitations of our past.

I recently read a piece by Bishop T. D. Jakes, who says, "Let Them Go!"

There are people who can walk away from you.
And hear me when I tell you this!
When people can walk away from you, let them walk.

*I don't want you to talk another person into staying with you, loving you,
    calling you, caring about you, coming to see you, staying attached to
    you.*
I mean, hang up the phone.
When people can walk away from you, let them walk.
Your destiny is never tied to anybody who left.

I promise you that as you surrender and let go of what you've
been holding on to, new people, inspiring people who see your
greatness, will show up in your life. It is in this peaceful, heartful
state of surrender that you can have what you want, know that it
is safe to speak out, and know that you are worthy of relaxing and
moving forward rather than staying stuck in a past that can never
be changed. When you learn that you can trust life, life will deliver treasures beyond your imagination. You will find the courage
and confidence that will remain with you every day for the rest of
your life.

And just as we need the Code of Divine Guidance to feel
that there is always a partner by our side, the Code of Surrender allows us to exhale and see ourselves beyond what we know
about ourselves. One of the many voices of surrender says, "Trust.
Trust. Trust that you were designed perfectly and that each experience has gotten you to a place where you can be your most
powerful self."

When Miyoko came to train with me, she wanted to find her
voice again—a voice that even during our phone calls was quiet,
meek, and timid. When I asked my students to look at the areas of
their lives where they felt stuck and faithless and to then focus on
one such area they needed to surrender, Miyoko raised her hand

to share. Stumbling over her words, she admitted to the group that there was a secret she had long been keeping, even from her fellow students in our intimate learning community. She shared that there is a part of her that is attracted to women. She went on to tell us that she'd known from a very young age that she had these feelings. When she was in high school, she even fell in love with a classmate. But then fear took over, and she stopped the relationship.

Miyoko knew that her family and her Japanese culture would disapprove. She had a clear idea of how hard it would be to be so different from those around her. In her mind, she had tried many times to imagine what it would be like, and it never got easier. She feared the judgment, the ridicule, and the stigma that would come along with being who she really was. She didn't trust in herself or in the feelings that resided deep within her. So Miyoko willed herself to ignore her feelings, to deny her impulses, and to do anything she could to kill off the part of her that was attracted to women. She focused all of her attention and energy on her education and then on her successful career in the biotechnology industry. She knew that something was missing from her life, but she rationalized that it was a small price to pay. She became rigid, controlling, and closed-minded as she fought off the inevitable attraction to women that would surface as she dated men and pursued a more traditional life.

Then one day, fifteen years later, as we embarked on the conversation about courage, Miyoko suddenly came face-to-face with this part of herself that she had so thoroughly rejected. She could see that she would need courage to be able to let this part of her live—and not only live but be loved—and she finally surrendered. Instead of fighting it, Miyoko opened her heart to the truth: that a part of her is attracted to women. When she surrendered, she was flooded with courage and confidence. She didn't have to conjure up courage and confidence; they simply arrived on the wave of her deep honesty.

Soon after, Miyoko invited a woman out on a date with her, and she even kissed her at the end of the night. She began to allow herself to imagine sharing her life with a woman. She confided in a cousin she was close to, only to find out that this cousin was a lesbian who had been hiding it from her family, too. Miyoko felt liberated and exhilarated, amazed that the life she had always wanted—one even greater than the one she had tried to create out of the sheer force of her will—unfolded only when she at last let go and surrendered.

The power of Miyoko's transformation is captured beautifully in Lao-tzu's simple observation "When I let go of what I am, I become what I might be."

When we surrender and let go, we must resign as general manager of the universe. We must mind our own business. We must stop believing that we are in control of everything. We must take our power where it lives—in this moment—and surrender to a path even if we don't know where the path is going. The hardest part of turning our lives over to the care of a power greater than ourselves and choosing surrender over control is that we have to resign from this lofty position. We have to give up our way of doing things, our efforts to control the situations and circumstances of our lives. We must let go of the things we believed to be true. The truth is that we really have no idea where the universe is trying to guide us. But wherever it is, I believe it's essential to stop and listen for the whispers that the Divine offers through its many different voices. The Voice of Courage, the Voice of a New Future, the Voice of Our Own Greatness will sneak in when all the activity stops—especially the activity of the mind, since our minds cannot take us where our hearts long to go.

THE SURRENDER PROCESS

Pick your favorite writing spot again, and settle in for a little quality time with your inner world. Take just a few clarifying minutes for personal reflection.

1. **What are you not accepting?** Make a list of any areas of your life where you're experiencing some conflict or inner resistance—where you're refusing to accept things as they actually are.

2. **The Voice of Control**: What does the Voice of Control say to you? Write out the negative internal dialogue that limits your ability to let go in any part of your life.

3. **When things were beyond your control**: Make a list of the times in your life when you tried to control circumstances and it didn't work. What default behaviors or strategies did you use? And what were the outcomes?

4. **The Voice of Surrender**: What does the Voice of Surrender tell you? You've probably heard its voice many times in

your life. Write out the wisdom and comfort that the Voice of Surrender whispers to you.

5. **Dear Universe:** Write a letter of resignation giving up your position as the general manager of the universe. And be sure to write down the specific date by which you will leave your post (note: the sooner, the better).

Courage Activator

Pick a song about courage as your personal anthem. Don't hold back. Allow yourself to sing and dance to it in the mirror every day. Even if you've never done this, it will activate your courage, so make sure that even if you're uncomfortable you take this step. Suggestions can be found at debbieford.com/courage.

Confidence Builder

Frame a picture of yourself as a young girl and put it by your bedside. Give her a positive, confidence-building message every day.

Courage and Confidence Bonus

Make a list of five risks you have taken in your life. Let yourself feel proud of your courage and confidence.

The Code of
Emotional Freedom

Emotional freedom is the doorway to our dreams and the goal of the warrior within. This warrior woman is the part of us standing for our greatness, our magnificence, and our joy. She is filled with the courage, confidence, and inner strength to leave the past behind. She knows that there is no way to express herself fully when she is still carrying burdens that need to be released. She won't settle for a reality that is dragged down by unfinished business. She embraces the present. Her strength returns even after the worst defeat because she has grown to trust herself. She is intensely honest with herself. Unwilling to have negativity or old fears stop her, she is strong, determined, and single-focused. Like an alchemist, she creates an elixir out of wisdom and courage to resolve any remnants of emotional toxicity. The warrior woman has found freedom.

Emotional freedom means embracing responsibility and accountability. To allow ourselves to move through our experiences instead of staying stuck in them, we look for how we participated in the circumstances, experiences, and conditions of our lives. As we embrace responsibility, we are given the gift of clear sight and are able to see how much we have grown and evolved from the experiences we have lived through.

Then, as we answer the following questions with sincerity, we move from powerlessness to empowerment, from victim to victor, from heaviness to lightness:

How can I learn from this?

What is the message I need to hear?

What is the gift that this experience holds for me?

What, if anything, do I need to do to unburden myself so I can move forward with grace, determination, and divine confidence?

The gift of taking responsibility for our journey allows us the kind of emotional freedom that can't be gotten anywhere else. We're able to see and claim for ourselves the immense inner strength always available to us.

So why is it that so many of us hold on to experiences from our past, refusing to let them go? Is it because we don't know how to let go and move on? Or could it be that our familiar emotional wounds are part of our story, our human drama, and we somehow feel more like ourselves when we're holding on to them?

To experience emotional freedom, we must accept, surrender, and let go of our wounds. We must be willing to take responsibility for what we're holding on to, which is usually a hurt or pain from the past that leaves us feeling victimized. The Code of Emotional Freedom calls on us to let go of "I'm right," "You're wrong," "I'm good," and "You're bad" so that we can stand fully in our power. It calls on us to take responsibility for our lives and then, with grace and ease, to let go of our excuses, reasons, justifications, and righteousness.

Now, that doesn't mean we're suddenly deaf, dumb, and blind to the impact that others have had on us. Becoming accountable doesn't mean letting the other person off the hook. As my friend Marianne Williamson always says, the universe will deal with them. But taking responsibility does guarantee that we will reclaim the power we have given away and regain our freedom to glide through the universe unobstructed by old beliefs or other people.

Holding back from taking full responsibility is common to all of us. Our wounded human ego wants to pin the blame on someone else—anyone else! Being a victim allows us to point our fingers and justify the condition of our lives. It gives us a way to explain why we don't have the strength or the courage we need to make changes.

Blame is a clever trickster. At its root, blame is a form of fear that helps us avoid accountability for our lives. We can be assured that every time we are blaming, we are casting ourselves in the role of the victim and somebody else in the role of the victimizer. But the underbelly of this victim mentality is that it winds up victimizing us as well. When we point our finger at someone else and say, "They lied to me" or "They cheated on me" or "They betrayed me," there is an accompanying internal dialogue that goes along with it: "How could I have let that happen?" Or "I should have stopped it." Or "I had the impulse to stay away and didn't." In this framework of blame, there's plenty of condemnation to go around. The pain and resentment that build over time from the experiences we feel victimized by prevent us from being able to digest and let go of our old emotional baggage. Instead, we stay stuck in the grip of fear.

The good news is that something magical happens when we own and embrace something we've avoided taking responsibility for in the past.

I experienced this in my own life when, five years into my career as a bestselling author, teacher, and leader in emotional and spiritual education, I found myself embroiled in a crisis with a group of consultants I had hired to run and operate my business. Even though we were thriving financially, problems frequently cropped up that I had no desire to deal with, and I was excited to find a team who could competently handle the details of my growing enterprise. When I hired them, they had promised me everything a fast-growing business needs—professionalism, full accounting and reporting, business planning, profitability, and 100 percent accountability for the business's success. I was delighted to be freed up from the day-to-day administration and management of the company.

I soon realized that the promises they made had been broken, when someone on my staff called to tell me she wouldn't be getting paid that week. I was appalled when I saw that the bank balance was dangerously low, the staff wasn't getting paid, and the finances were in the worst condition they had ever been in. Although there was much confusion as to how the consultants were managing the distribution of funds, it was very easy to see the hundred thousand–plus dollars they had taken for themselves. Of course when I called them, they blamed everybody else, taking no responsibility whatsoever. Listening to them on the other end of the phone, I felt angry, frustrated, and powerless. All I could think of was how I had been screwed yet again.

Unfortunately, this wasn't the first time I had found myself in this mess. In fact, I had handed my business over on a silver platter three different times before this. My pattern was that I would find a man or company to manage my business and be 100 percent accountable for its success. If I liked them and felt good around them, nothing else seemed to matter. I would get caught up in the promises they made and the vision they had for a fabulous future because it already was a thriving business. *What could go wrong?* I thought. *No one would want to derail a company doing such valuable work in the world.*

But then I would be snapped out of my fantasy. Inevitably things would fall apart. They would spend more money than what was coming in, and I would find myself picking up the pieces. It never took much to clean things up—a testament to the service my business was providing to the large numbers of people who enrolled in our workshops and training programs. All it required was that I take back the reins of my business and meet regularly with the staff. Usually within three months, whatever issues there were would get cleaned up. Then, three or four weeks later, I'd start searching for the next person or company that could take the management of the business off my hands and relieve me of the pressure I felt. And each time things fell apart, all I could think about was the famous quote "Insanity is doing the same thing over and over and expecting different results." That was me. I was definitely doing the same thing over and over again, and each time I was expecting a different result.

Even though everybody wanted to give me their opinions and valuable advice, I was committed to being right (even if I was horribly wrong), and there wasn't anyone who dared cross that boundary except my mother. She handled all my personal finances and often my business finances when I took it back from the hands of consultants—which gave her a unique window into my insanity as it unfolded. Even though I would tell her, "I don't want to hear what you have to say," she would slip it in there anytime she could. "Why did you hire these people? I knew they were going to do this. You have *sucker* stamped across your forehead. They have no idea what they're doing. They're idiots." But instead of being angry at the people who were messing with my business and leaving me in a compromised position, I would get mad at my mom, like it was her fault. I made her wrong. What did she know? I can tell you one thing: she knew that I was working eighteen hours a day and that other people were taking my money. That's what she knew.

The trauma, pain, and upset of this pattern gave me plenty of ammo for beating myself up. It cost me my peace of mind and the freedom to enjoy all the amazing things that were happening in my life and career. It cost me the opportunity to take time off and just be present with my son. It cost me the desire to trust other people. It robbed me of the ability to be in the presence of all the miracles that were taking place in the lives of the people who were training with us. When others observed my business and the transformation that occurs for people as a result of it, they wanted to soak it up and dwell in it. Instead I always wanted to run from it.

By this time, I had to look at why, despite all this evidence, I was so resistant to managing and being accountable for my own business and its money. How could I be so successful and so stupid at the same time? And why would I—without knowing much about someone, but because I felt a connection with that person—hand over the keys to the safe to him? Why was I so resistant to taking responsibility for managing a business that was fulfilling my life's mission? All I ever wanted to do was train leaders to be who they are at their core, to stand strong in the middle of controversy, to take risks even though they're scared, and to let their magnificence and power shine. So why did I resent the pressure I felt in fulfilling my mission?

No excuses could absolve me from the need to see that this was something I had to deal with. No layers of denial could shield me from the reality that if I didn't make a radical change, the stress was going to kill me—literally—because it had already taken my energy, my joy, and my happiness away from me. So I did what I would coach anyone to do—some serious soul searching. I asked one of my staff coaches to take me through one of our processes. As she had me close my eyes and look back into my history, she wanted me to call forth a memory that was causing my resistance.

In my mind, I could see my mother dressed beautifully, getting ready for work as she got us ready for school. She was very young when she got married, and at some point she decided that she could no longer fit into the mold of a 1960s stay-at-home mom. She became a great pioneer and leader among the other women in our town. She was one of the only mothers I knew who got a job, decided she wanted a divorce (which no one at the time was doing), and got the training she needed to become an insurance agent. She became a successful businesswoman and a powerful presence in her field.

As these memories of my mother came to me, I could begin to feel the conflicting emotions within me. On the one hand, I felt proud of the choices that my mother had made. But then I also remembered being so young and feeling ashamed and embarrassed that I had a mother who was so different, a mother who wasn't there when I got home from school every day, making me cookies. I was surprised by the shame and embarrassment I felt back then, and it sparked realizations about my own inner conflicts about being a working mother. I began to think about some of the guilty feelings I was experiencing in having a young son at home and at the same time being on the road, being very committed to my career, and seemingly being able to take it all on. People around me would say, "You're the strongest woman I know," even though I could see that in the running of the business I felt weak, powerless, and overwhelmed.

Today I would brag to you about how my mother wound up owning her own insurance agency; how she was one of the first women to work with Lloyd's of London; how she learned to fly an airplane; how she became a gourmet cook; and on and on. But for a long time I wasn't able to reconcile the conflicting feelings I carried about my mother's choices. Inevitably, I had made conflicting decisions that were showing up as contradictions in my life. I was a working mom, just like my mother, and yet I was fighting against that reality. She was totally into running a business, and I was totally against it. I came to the realization that I set up the same situation time and time again because I wanted someone to save me. I wanted somebody else to be responsible, to be the driver, and just report to me how great everything was going. And as I looked even deeper, I unearthed my belief that a *man* needed to run my business in order for it to succeed.

Standing in the truth that I had been the one to create these repeated disasters with my business, that I was responsible, I suddenly had the deeper insight that responsibility brings. I could see that I was not just caught up in a pattern in which my appointed saviors were screwing me. I had screwed myself by not taking any responsibility for running my business. I had drawn into my world people who had conflicting motives, people who really didn't care or didn't know how to run my business. *Mom, you were right.* I was the one who kept giving away my power like a hot potato that I couldn't toss quickly enough to someone else.

As soon as I took responsibility for the choices I'd made, I knew I had to take my power back as a woman, secure in my belief that it is okay for women to be great business leaders. My feelings of stress and inadequacy started to melt away. My staff became a more cohesive team. We found the perfect person to handle the financial reporting for the business. As our vision began to grow, running the business ceased to be a chore and instead became a place for me to contribute to the world. This was the beautiful gift of taking responsibility—one that has positively affected the lives of thousands of people around the world.

Looking back, I can see that blame kept me feeling bad and trapped in a position of powerlessness. The only way for me to reclaim my power and heal my heart was to take 100 percent responsibility for all of my choices and circumstances. It was this taking responsibility that granted me true freedom and the ability to walk out of the prison of being victimized by this pattern. Although the tricky voice of my ego warned me, "It's really not your fault. You're a victim," my willingness to be accountable and honest with myself gave me a new vantage point.

We must trust that everything in the universe is guiding us to a higher place. We must accept that if we have an emotionally based behavior pattern that we don't own up to or can't see, we will repeat that pattern. We must surrender our excuses, justifications, rationalizations, and the fear that created them. We must recognize that our way of holding on instead of letting go has seen its day, and then willingly surrender managing these experiences. With this newly "retrofitted" foundation, we can confidently take full responsibility for co-creating our lives, opening the door to emotional freedom.

Taking responsibility means taking ownership. It means acknowledging that we have in fact participated (even if on an unconscious level) in the choices and actions that brought about the most painful events we have gone through. This is alarming only if we are not standing in the knowledge that we are living our intended life—the life that brings us the experiences perfectly suited to our becoming the women we have always wanted to be.

When we take 100 percent responsibility, we take responsibility not just for the circumstances of our lives but for our emotions and our internal world as well. We can't heal what we can't feel. In order to take back our power and regain control of our lives, we must take ownership of our emotions. This requires that we acknowledge and own the depth of our hurt and pain. Our painful emotions can push us back into the small, defensive, resistant shell of our old emotional wounds. The disappointments, grudges, and resignation stemming from past betrayals may come up and drive us to retreat and protect ourselves. But the Code of Emotional Freedom promises us that we are safe to let go of our struggle and our distrustful behaviors. Once we can recognize that we're trapped in the limited reality of our hurts, we have a choice. We can choose to continue to allow our thoughts, words, and actions to be driven by fear, or we can choose to be guided by courage. With courage as our compass, not only do we take responsibility for our lives in the present, but we take responsibility for our futures as well.

In taking responsibility, stepping out of blame and victimization, and beginning to heal our inner world, we are able to ensure that we don't unconsciously attract the same kinds of people, circumstances, and events that previously left us feeling victimized. How many of us have dated the same kind of person, had the same kind of boss, kept making the same mistakes over and over again? If we do not identify how we participate in these experiences and own up to our part, we will continue to repeat the pattern over and over again. It's difficult to recognize a problem coming toward us unless we can recognize the issue inside of us.

Often, the issues that remain the most painful and hang around our necks like a two-ton anchor are set off by a belief that is waiting and wanting to be healed. Such beliefs are hidden—out of our sight and beyond our conscious awareness. But although they're hidden, they still dictate our behavior. I call these beliefs Shadow Beliefs. When we are unwilling or unable to take responsibility for our lives, we can be sure of one thing: there is some unconscious belief driving our choices.

Melanie, a fifty-eight-year-old mother of two, came to the Shadow Process Retreat, my three-day workshop that promises to transform any area of pain and loss into success and happiness, to address her relationship. I noticed her one morning when she was emphatically raising her hand, trying to get my attention. When I called on her and she stood, her voice was shaking, and the microphone shook in her hand. She put the microphone to her lips and said, "I'm going to get divorced." I could see the disbelief cross her face as she heard her own words amplified in the room. She repeated, "I've been married for almost forty years, and I'm going to get a divorce." When I asked Melanie why she was leaving her marriage, she launched into a diatribe about her husband, Steve. She described his emotional and verbal abuse and the way he neglected her and their children. She blamed him for her unhappiness and described the weight she had gained and the drugs and alcohol she'd consumed just to be able to stay in the marriage this long. As she ranted on and on about her husband, I stopped her and asked, "Why did you choose to marry him?" And she whispered quietly, "Well, I didn't want to." Then she went on to tell us her story.

Melanie was eighteen years old on the day of her wedding. It was a bright, sunny spring day, and she was adorned in her wedding dress like a fairy princess, looking beautiful and waiting for the man of her dreams to enter the room. She heard him coming up the stairs and was breathless with anticipation, having decided to set her doubts aside to make this the most magical day of her life. Hearing his voice as he opened the door brought a big smile to her face. As she looked up to give him a warm, loving hello and embrace, Steve, without a glance, hurriedly walked by Melanie, not even acknowledging her presence. Her heart sank, her joy vanished in an instant, and an overwhelming sense of gloom filled her entire being. Melanie heard a voice screaming in her head, "Get up! Get out! You need to run away!" But Melanie couldn't move. In complete devastation, she sat there paralyzed, frozen to her chair. As minutes went by with Steve still ignoring her, Melanie tried to think of how she could get out of this. What could she do? She thought about how her parents had taken out a loan for the wedding. She thought about all her friends and family who had arrived to celebrate her seemingly good fortune. She thought about her mother, who told her over and over again that a woman is only as good as the man she marries. Her mother would say, "If you're a good woman, you'll get a good man." With each thought of why she couldn't get out of it, she became more and more resigned to being the good girl. She told herself that Steve was just nervous and that it would all be okay. As she took her father's arm and walked down the aisle, she plastered on her best "I'm so happy, joyful, and in love" face, but inside she wanted to die. The night got better for her as people drank, danced, and celebrated the newlyweds, but reality set in again days later as the couple moved into their home.

As Melanie told us the story, tears ran down her face. I could actually hear the shame, the pain, the loss, and the heartache of the beautiful young woman she was on her wedding day. Melanie stood there in shock as she admitted that she had never told this story to anyone. And when I suggested to Melanie that she had now exposed where she participated in this dysfunctional and abusive relationship, she said she had never thought about that before. But now she could see that pivotal moment of choice. She saw that she had a choice to turn around and run or to succumb, and that she chose to succumb and become the victim. For forty years, she participated in her own self-sabotage over and over again. Standing there in the safety of the seminar room, she realized that it was now or never; that if she was going to reclaim her passion, her vibrancy, and find any sort of happiness for her future, she would have to take responsibility for her choices and be accountable for the beliefs that had driven them. In taking responsibility, Melanie could finally access the courage she needed to leave her husband, the freedom to support herself and make her own decisions, and the trust in herself and her relationship with the Divine.

I can see her today, laughing so hard, realizing that she had given up so much of her power in blaming him when she could have owned up to her part and moved on anytime she wanted. On the day of her divorce, Melanie wrote me a note saying, "I've finally set myself free."

By looking through the eyes of co-creation—seeing that we are co-creating this universe, co-creating our relationships, and co-creating our experiences—we can find the unseen patterns that exist inside of us. And with this clear-eyed wisdom, we are able to cut the line, drop the anchor, and set ourselves free. Released from the past, we are gifted with the emotional freedom to be the courageous women we were designed to be.

THE EMOTIONAL FREEDOM PROCESS

Put on a little relaxing music if you'd like. Bring out your journal. And with a calming and connecting deep breath, open up to answering the following questions:

1. **Acknowledging your inner victim:** Make a list of the situations in your life where you are blaming, pointing your finger, holding on to anger, and feeling like a victim.

2. **Identifying the biggest blockage:** On the list you just made, circle the three situations that most stand in the way of your courage and your confidence.

3. **Claiming your part in the drama:** Journal about whether you had a role in these dramas. What was your role in them? What choices did you make that put you in these

situations? Please make a commitment not to blame or berate yourself. If you're looking only at a place where you've been victimized, begin with an easier situation.

4. **Finding the gifts**: Answer the following questions about this challenging situation:

   • How can I learn from this?

   • What is the message I need to hear?

   • What is the gift that this experience holds for me?

5. **Freeing yourself**: Take an action that will support you in letting go of any baggage related to these three situations so that you can move forward with grace, determination, and divine confidence.

Courage Activator

Heal the people pleaser within you. Say no to at least three people who make a request of you, and affirm to yourself that it's perfectly safe to say no. Enjoy! Do this as many times as you can in the next six weeks. "No" is your friend.

Confidence Builder

Go out in the world and get rejected three times. Purposely make requests (ask for favors, help, money, participation in something, and so on) that you're sure will get turned down. You might ask somebody who is overly busy but has a great restaurant to come to your house to cook dinner for you and your family. Or ask somebody who hates to loan money to lend you fifty thousand dollars for four months. If they ask why, tell them it's none of their business. Then, when they refuse, say, "Thank you for allowing me to ask." Don't tell them that it's your homework! This is a potent opportunity to affirm that it's okay for people to say no to you.

Courage and Confidence Bonus

Make a list of seven situations in which you told the truth even though you didn't want to.

The Code of Heartful Compassion

You have the power to bring a new, profound understanding and appreciation to your past and all the experiences you've had. I am going to suggest that you needed these experiences to be who you want to be in the world—for yourself, for your family, for your community, and for humanity. The perfect people and the perfect experiences have shown up in your life. You have had the perfect family for you to learn, grow, and evolve. It is only the Voice of Fear, in all its persistent yammering, that obscures these truths and attempts to diminish the power of the life you have lived. To silence the Voice of Fear, you need only reach a hand toward the beautiful unknown and call on heartful compassion to believe that there is a profound meaning to all that you have lived, even the darkest moments.

The Code of Heartful Compassion is birthed out of the belief that there is a greater reason for everything. There is a design for your life that is worth fighting for, a plan that holds profound meaning beyond your ego's ability to understand. This code invites you to know and embrace this larger reality by stepping out of your limited perspective and into the worldview that there are no accidents and that everything is happening for a reason, even when you can't see it. This view is life changing in and of itself, because it takes you out of "Why me?"; "Poor me"; "It shouldn't be"; "Why is this happening?"; "Why did this happen?"; or "It's all their fault"—any one of which then turns into blame. When your inner judge begins to find evidence to hold on to the hurt that keeps you rooted in the past, filled with resentments or grudges, you are prohibited from feeling your compassionate heart.

The Voice of Fear insists that the challenges you have gone through permanently scarred you. And the cost of listening to your fear can probably be most clearly seen in the patterns that plague you, whether they be repetitive cycles of self-sabotage, addiction, or relationship conflicts with lovers, friends, coworkers, or family members. These patterns might show up on your body or in your finances. But the steepest cost of all is that they undermine your courage and your confidence.

To enter the state of heartful compassion, we must search out and find what is weighing us down in the form of resentments and grudges. But for many of us, this requires that we first awaken from our denial. We often forget that we're holding this undigested anger as we distract ourselves with the pleasurable addictions that obscure the emotional truth. These are the habits and cravings that leave us with nothing more than short-lived feel-good moments rather than the long-term inner peace that we seek. And even if we are keenly aware that we're carrying grudges and resentments toward our exes, our bosses, or certain family members, we seem to use this knowledge as a defense mechanism. It becomes a shield that we use to build up a false sense of confidence and make ourselves feel better, all the while oblivious to the true cost of harboring these grudges.

We cannot have an open heart while we are carrying the burdens of the past. We cannot allow ourselves to experience our own grace and ease when we have our hearts closed to any part of the world. And we need not wait, as most do, until our death—whether it be an emotional, spiritual, or physical death—to drop the rocks of the negative feelings we're harboring toward others. Most of us have many rocks, many grudges. We can let ourselves be weighed down by the rocks of resentments from our past, or we can drop them through the power of forgiveness. The choice is ours.

Many of us have read about and talked about forgiveness, and we understand intellectually why it might benefit us to let go of anger toward others. But we hold on anyway. Sometimes we think that by holding on to our grudges, we'll get our revenge and make the other person pay for how they hurt us. But this just isn't what will happen. A wise person once wrote, "Resentment is like drinking poison and hoping the other person would die." But the only one dying is ourselves.

Kathy walked into the Shadow Process Retreat in her favorite Juicy Couture pink sweat suit, her long, beautiful flowing hair swaying down her back—a head-turner for sure. Yet despite all her feminine swagger as she entered the room, she couldn't conceal the devastation, hurt, and rage written all over her face. What had she endured? What experience had stolen her true self-confidence? She sat in the very front row with a seriousness that penetrated right through me. Everyone comes into the Shadow Process with some heartache, some hurt, some dark secret that they want to unload. But I could tell by the questions she asked and the notes she was taking that she was a deep thinker; she was unusually articulate and persuasive at arguing the case for her past. I later found out that she was a lawyer.

As the weekend went on, all I could think was "This woman hates me." I was quite sure that she hated how I kept raising the possibility that ultimately every horrific experience comes bearing great gifts. Eventually it came to a boiling point. Unwilling to accept this idea, Kathy stood up to argue her case. As with any good lawyer, she had collected tons of evidence that there was nothing divine or good or even okay with what she had just gone through. She was the wronged party. That was her story and she was sticking to it. Case closed. I proceeded to tell her that she could go home with her resentment and rage intact, but it wasn't going to make her feel any better or change any outcomes.

Kathy's story went something like this.

Kathy and her husband were, by all appearances, the perfect power couple. Everybody wanted to run in their circle and emulate their glamorous life as a loving couple and family. Kathy was twenty-seven when she married Stuart, a man fifteen years older than she, someone who she believed was trustworthy, dependable, and generous—someone who surely would take care of her the way her father had. But after they had been together only a few short years, Stuart slowly began turning into a monster that she didn't recognize. The clues began to accumulate. Over the years, he wouldn't show up for his three gorgeous daughters' school plays or music recitals, for family dinners, or even to kiss his daughters goodnight. Even though he knew the girls were waiting for him, Stuart never showed up for them. His drinking became a problem, and he seemed to always embarrass Kathy in public, whether it was fighting for the keys after dinner out, groping a woman in a French maid's costume at a Halloween party, or getting drunk and being unwilling to say anything nice about his daughters at their b'nai mitzvah. In fact, when he did get the microphone that afternoon, he barely acknowledged his daughters, wasting those precious few minutes babbling on about one of the other kids at the party, the son of another couple.

Of course, then the cheating began. Kathy would wait every night for him to come home, rejecting the notion that he would ever go that far. But when women started calling the house, she knew she'd better open her eyes.

Then the day came when someone told her that she might want to read a website that Stuart's disgruntled employees had put up online to expose him. Feeling nauseated, she pulled herself together, closed the doors, and sat in front of the computer, waiting to muster up the courage to look at the site. When she opened it, what she found was worse than anything she could imagine. A former employee had posted a message that read, "It's too bad he's such a scumbag. He's got such a great wife. Do you think she knows that he's cheating on her with her close friend Barbara? In fact the last time I was in his office, she was under his desk." When Kathy read that it wasn't only her husband betraying her but also one of her closest friends, someone who came to her house regularly for dinner and family events, it tore open such deep pain and hurt that she didn't know what to do with her feelings. So she continued to do what was familiar: she stuffed the blinding anguish down as far as possible and painted on a happy face.

Then came the final straw—Thanksgiving dinner at her sister's house. Everybody knew that Thanksgiving dinner was very important to Kathy's parents, so the family dressed impeccably to show their respect. Their daughters looked beautiful; Kathy looked beautiful. Even Stuart had dressed up for the night and looked like the man she thought she had married. En route to the car, he stopped her, took her arm, and, turning her toward him, said, "I'm not going to your sister's tonight unless you write me a check right now for half a million dollars." Her jaw dropped. Not knowing what to say or do, with the girls waiting in the car, Kathy thought about what would be more horrible—giving him more money in his latest blackmail attempt, or having to explain once again to her family why Stuart wasn't coming to dinner on such an important night. With hot tears burning her eyes, Kathy returned to the foyer, pulled her checkbook out of her purse, and wrote him a check for five hundred thousand dollars. As she handed Stuart the check, completely filled with shame, Kathy calculated that she had given or lent this man over three million dollars, and he still treated her like a piece of crap. She realized she was trying to buy the love he wouldn't freely give her. Even though she had been determined to stay in the marriage to save face and to have her children grow up with a father, the emotional abuse was now more than she could handle.

Collectively holding our breath as she recounted the horror, the whole group of us in the workshop had to take a big exhale after hearing Kathy's story. It was hard to believe that this had happened to anybody, but especially to this woman, who was obviously strong, confident, well educated, and worldly. I reassured Kathy that she had a right to be angry, resentful, and hurt. Certainly that would be a healthy first response. After hearing just the first few stories, even I was ready to take a knife to him. She had endured a kind of persecution that none of us should ever have to go through. I didn't want to minimize her pain or the tremendous hurt that broke her heart, but for the next step to happen, she would have to look at what holding on to her anger and resentment was costing her.

Kathy acknowledged that she couldn't get into a relationship with another man. In fact, she couldn't even have dinner with a man without thinking about how he was going to betray her. It cost her being a role model for her girls, who were the most important thing in the world to her. They had started seeing her as a victim as they watched her repeatedly cower under their father's domination. Now they had the victim/victimizer dynamic firmly imprinted on their psyches. Her anger and resentment cost her her joy, her emotional freedom, and the ability to fully appreciate how lucky she was to be born into a wonderful family who had enough money to set her up for life. All she could think about

was how she had given so much of it away. When she truly realized the cost—on her life, on her children's lives, on the future of
her loving family—Kathy broke down in tears. She had lost her
dream marriage. She had lost her dignity. She had lost her faith.
But as she now allowed the hurt to be there, the anger subsided
and she gradually started opening her heart to herself, to the
sweet woman she was, a woman who had tried very hard to hold
her family together.

Now it was time to see whether Kathy was willing to open up
her heart to compassion. This was a big leap for somebody who
had been through so much betrayal. So I asked Kathy to momentarily suspend what she believed about her life and to envision a
brand-new reality. I asked her to stand in a place where the whole
universe was loving her, where her highest self was cheering her
on, where she could see only what was good and could find the
gifts in her experience. I asked her to close her human eyes and
look at her life through the eyes of heartful compassion. What
did she see? The first thing she saw was how hurt and wounded
Stuart was and how everything that he had done was an effort to
make himself feel better because he felt so inadequate around her.

Through the eyes of compassion, she could see how much she
had learned about denial and the true cost of it. Kathy could also
see she had learned about financial responsibility for the first time
since inheriting money from her family—a lesson she hadn't had
to learn before. Until the nightmare with Stuart unfolded, Kathy
wasn't aware of how ashamed and guilty she felt about being rich.
She also wasn't aware of how ashamed she felt about the state of
her marriage. She had been living a secret life that separated her

from her family so she wouldn't have to expose the terrible truth that her husband wanted her money. The greatest gift she could see through the eyes of compassion was the powerful example she was now setting for her three daughters about how to take care of themselves and not wait for their prince to ride in on a white horse like their mommy had done. She had learned through all of her experiences that money could be replaced but that the love she had with her children was irreplaceable.

Now we were at the moment of truth. I asked Kathy, "Are you brave enough, strong enough, and courageous enough to cut the cord of resentment, to drop the rock?" She closed her eyes to find the answer to my question, and then she said, in a very soft, open voice, "I am. I am courageous enough to let go of this." With that verbal commitment, I asked her to imagine that this whole life she had lived with Stuart was shrinking down to the size of the fingernail on her pinky finger. It would just be a tiny piece of her history.

Today, Kathy is living an amazing life. After going through my advanced training programs to become a coach and transformational leader, Kathy found a passion that could only have been birthed from her particular experience of marriage and divorce. She is profoundly inspired to be out in the world speaking about the work of Spiritual Divorce, based on my second book, and helping women transform their own divorce experience into a powerful catalyst for an extraordinary life. Free of her resentment and bitterness, she has tapped into the ability to help other women rise up from the ashes of the past.

At the very heart of Kathy's healing and transformation was the forgiveness she finally found for herself and even for Stuart. It didn't happen instantly, but the process truly set her free from the bondage of yesterday.

For every one of us, the practice of forgiveness is vital for the healing of our hearts so that we become willing to open up to an even greater level of divine connection. This sacred source is the very wellspring of our love, our courage, and our confidence. It is the love that transports us to a place where our hearts are pure, where we're not holding anything against anyone because we know that the universe has brought us the perfect people and experiences for our soul's evolution, allowing us to reconnect and live as divine messengers.

Although we "know" that all of our experiences are ultimately trying to lead us to open up and love, this is a conclusion we must finally reach with our hearts, not our heads. When we are holding on to any grudge, any resentment, any anger, any blame, any guilt, any regret, any judgment, any bitterness, any disappointment, any self-righteousness, any hate, or any revenge, it becomes a barrier between us and our loving hearts. When we are blocked from heartful compassion, we are unable to be the divine messenger that we are here to be, because our resentments are keeping us stuck with one foot in the past. If we are going to move forward as warriors of love—as women of courage, strength, and power—we cannot let incidents from our past bring us down for too long. We must release others—and, most important, ourselves—from the prison of the past.

As renowned medium James Van Praagh says, "We see these things as horrific experiences, terrible experiences, dark experiences, when in truth they are really enlightened experiences, because they help us to be who we are."

When we're going through continuous pain and harboring resentments, it's because we have attached negative interpretations and feelings to the experiences we've had and are unwilling to give them up. It is our interpretations of events that continue to either hurt us or empower us. The meanings we choose to assign to the painful events of our lives have the power to either ground us in the past or support us in charging forward into our future.

When we comprehend the real cost of holding on to any kind of grudge or resentment, we can begin to make the more powerful choice to forgive. The costs are steep, but the results literally change the entire direction of our lives. It's crucial to take inventory of what our resentments are robbing us of and how they're depleting our power and light.

Holding on to resentments and grudges does the following:

Lowers our self-esteem
Separates us from ourselves
Keeps us disempowered and living in the past
Prevents us from healing underlying wounds
Keeps us a victim
Undermines our confidence
Makes us guarded instead of open
Drains our energy
Hardens us
Makes us old, angry, and tired
Causes stress

Diminishes our courage
Robs us of fulfilling relationships
Blinds us to new opportunities
Compromises our health

And the list goes on and on.

Our grudges and resentments can literally rob us of our greatest desires. One of my longtime students, Angie—a beautiful, sweet thirty-eight-year-old woman—brings a smile to everyone's face but was always complaining that she couldn't find a man to be in a relationship with. It made no logical sense to me. I had known her for a long time and had seen that everyone who met her fell in love with her. After hearing her complain one more time, I suggested that this had to be tied to an earlier event in her life, because there was no way that there weren't thousands of men who would want to scoop her up. I asked Angie to look into her past and find the first negative experience she could remember having with a man. She told me this story.

"When I was fifteen, I got my first job—working at a golf and tennis store. I loved sports and was thrilled about working and being able to make my own money. After a few weeks, my boss, Rob, who was about twenty-five years older than me, started making comments about how pretty I was, how special I was, and how glad he was that I was there by his side. Even though these were words I loved to hear because they made me feel confident and strong for a minute or two, the way he looked at me made me feel uncomfortable. Rob started sharing with me some very

intimate stories about his relationship with his wife and how un-
happy he was about being married to her. He would get himself
all worked up, saying she was a bitch and a bulldog. I just listened,
wondering why he kept telling me the details of his marriage.

"As time went on, Rob gave me more and more responsibility. He would leave the store, telling me he was going to give a
private tennis lesson and that if his wife called, I was to say he
had gone out on store business. Of course I knew he was out
with other women. And then one day he started to tell me about
these other women that he was sleeping with. I just tried to
ignore the information, because I wanted to keep my job. Every
time Rob crossed my boundaries, he would buy me a gift—a bi-
cycle, clothes, more money on my paycheck, and other random
presents. Then, an unpredictable thing happened. One day Rob
called me into the back of the store.

"I had a bad feeling, like something strange was going on. I
started to feel sick and hesitant but went back anyway. When I
stepped into the back office, I found Rob with his shorts down
around his ankles, fondling himself. I couldn't believe what he was
doing as he turned to me and said, 'Come on over here. Do you
want to touch me?' Appalled, I said, 'No!' Rob could see the disgust on my face and quickly said, 'Don't worry about it. You don't
have to touch me. Just watch me.' So I did. I kept my mouth shut,
feeling slimy and sick. I was so ashamed and humiliated. I didn't
have anybody to tell. I decided I would just wear bigger clothes so
men wouldn't look at me like a sexual object. I started drinking to
cover the pain of feeling disgusting and unlovable."

As Angie shared her story and became fully present to this burden she had carried and the grudge that was buried deep inside her, she was flooded with emotion. She realized that this one incident had affected all of her intimate relationships with men for the past twenty-three years. Angie admitted that this experience, which had stolen her youthful innocence, made her feel dirty with men to this day. Without a doubt, this was Angie's underlying issue. It was clear that she needed to find closure so that she could move on, create new relationships, and attract men who would respect and honor her. So I asked Angie to write a letter to Rob and not to hold anything back because she wouldn't be mailing it. I asked her to write down what the Voice of Blame had to say, because it was now time to let go, drop her rock, and move on. When Angie read me her letter, I could hear the protective venom and power in her voice. She was finally dealing with a resentment she didn't even know she harbored.

Rob,

You have taken the deepest part of my soul and violated me with your sick and twisted, sexually deviant behavior. You made me feel so worthless, disgusting, and dirty. And since those sick and perverted moments when you made me watch you masturbate, I have believed that no man would ever want to come near me. You took advantage of me with your sick mind, making me think that I was so special and important, when all along you just wanted me for your pleasure and satisfaction. You are a predator, and I wish I would have turned you in. I feel so much hate for you. I hate you for controlling me and making me feel like your

prostitute, only good for your sick and twisted pleasure. How could you
rob me of feeling like a normal teenager? I hate you for this. You're a
SICK, FUCKED UP MAN. I HOPE YOU ROT IN HELL.

Angie

After she read her letter, I asked Angie if she was ready to cut the cord and let her resentment go. To do this, she would need to accept that Rob was a sick man and that she had unfortunately gotten caught up in his sickness. She would need to see that although what he did was wrong, if she was ever going to find the true intimate love she was looking for, she would have to be present to the Voice of Heartful Compassion. This would be the healing balm that would allow her heart to receive the gifts that this experience had the potential to give her. As Angie took some slow, deep breaths, I asked her to tell me what the Voice of Heartful Compassion wanted to say to her. Tuning in, Angie heard:

Forgive so that your heart can grow bigger and softer.
You will be taken care of by the Divine.
You don't need to be afraid to open your heart and surrender.
You can let go of this incident.
Find the love within your heart. It is there calling to you.
Let go and let God's love fill your heart and guide you.
All your stories and pain have made you the woman that you are today.
Be grateful for every second of your past.
Be a beacon of light in the dark.
Believe in me.
You are safe with the Divine.

Listening to the Voice of Heartful Compassion changed Angie's view of this incident, and her life as a whole. She felt lighter, happier, more spontaneous, and in the presence of her compassionate heart.

Now it was time for her to claim the gifts—the lessons and the wisdom—of this experience. She had learned to respect herself and trust her instincts. She became committed to teaching and training young teenage girls about how to take care of themselves. She had a deep compassion for people who had been sexually abused or inappropriately touched. As she claimed one gift after another, I heard an undeniable confidence in her voice and the love song that emanated from her heart.

When we let compassion change us the way Angie let it change her, we experience deep and unlimited peace. Our perceptions are refined, and we are given the ability to see people differently. We become attuned to the Divine and aligned with a newfound source of happiness, joy, love, courage, and confidence.

Basking in the humility of our soul's mission here on earth, we are released from the unchanging story line of the wounded ego and are able to see new possibilities for the contributions we are here to make. Holding grudges and blaming are acts of the ego, while surrender and forgiveness are acts of the Divine. In each moment, this is the choice we make: to align either with our ego or with the divine love that brought us to the world. As our hearts open, we step into the grace and flow of the miracles that life is offering us never-endingly.

THE HEARTFUL COMPASSION PROCESS

Set aside your projects and to-do list for a few minutes, pull out your journal, and settle in for a life-transforming period of inner reflection.

1. **Admitting to your grudges:** Close your eyes, take a deep breath, and let any grudges or resentments you're holding on to come into your awareness. Make a list. What are the hurts or betrayals that you haven't gotten over?

2. **Dampening your courage and confidence:** Make a list of what it costs you to hold on to resentments and grudges. How does it affect your health, energy, time, creativity, and joy? More specifically, how does it diminish your courage and your confidence?

3. **The one big resentment:** Pick the one resentment or grudge that most stands in the way of your being a confident, courageous warrior of love.

4. **The uncensored story:** Write out the story of this experience in all its dramatic and gory detail.

5. **Getting it off your chest:** Write a blame letter to the person who wronged you, venting all of your anger and resentment toward him or her. No holding back. (Don't worry, you won't send it.)

6. **The Voice of Heartful Compassion:** Tune in to the Voice of Heartful Compassion and write down what it wants to say to you about this situation. Listen to what it has to tell

you about the wisdom and the gifts you have gained from this experience.

7. **Forgive**: Take an action this week that will support you in releasing the burden of this resentment and in opening yourself up to life in a bigger way.

Courage Activator

Communicate to someone something that you have been scared to express . . . and with no attachment to whether or not they like it. Share your blame letter with a compassionate friend.

Confidence Builder

Make a list of all of the blessings, gifts, and grace in your life. Write down at least ten things you're grateful for, and then add one each day.

Courage and Confidence Bonus

List five times in your life when you admitted you were wrong.

The Code of a Loving Heart

Self-love is the warrior's code. It is the source of her courage and her confidence. When she is present and awake to all that she is, she is able to take on any challenge, any project, or any future that she desires. Her heart wants to serve, protect, love, and heal all those who come onto her path. She is smart enough to know that anything that is holding her back will only slow her down or send her off in a direction that doesn't lead to the fulfillment of her dreams. Her daily prayer is to have the strength to love all of herself, the courage to listen to what she is guided to do, and the confidence to go out, stand tall, and deliver her gifts to the world. The present moment is her source of great inspiration. Because her intention and focus are clear, she can open up to who she is and who she desires to be.

When you are not complete with the past, you drag it around with you wherever you go, using it as a reference point for who you are, for what you think, for what you believe, and for the choices you make. Unknowingly, you dip into your past experiences, which are usually telling you what you can or cannot do. Instead of standing in the present moment and looking to a future that you're thrilled and excited about, you sit there and listen to the same conversations whirling around in your mind. So, knowing this, how could you expect your future to be much different from your past when you are actually going to the past (without even realizing it) to decide who you are and what you're capable of? In these defining moments—when you need all your courage, strength, and the highest vision of who you are—you bring your limitations from the past into the present and then project them into the future.

For example, you decide to finally speak your truth to a friend who is always sapping your energy. The first thing you might think is "I've said this before. I've tried to say it. I'll hurt her feelings. It's not a nice thing to do. Just keep your mouth shut. You'll be better off." And then, like a coward, you give your power away. You don't say the thing you know you need to say, thinking it's safer that way, since that's what you learned in the past. You project the feelings of the self that you were in the past onto this moment and make your decision from there, which then, of course, affects your future, your self-esteem, and your confidence. The ripple effect is set in motion. You allow your fearful self to make your choices instead of having the courage and confidence to make a new, fresh choice based on who you are today and who you want to be in the future. This course of action is predictable when you are incomplete with your past.

Completion is an important part of learning to love yourself at a whole new level. To me, completion is so exciting because you are literally making a choice to leave the past behind. You are drawing a line in the sand. There may be letters to write, conversations to be had, and closure to experience. And you are fiercely directed in your actions. Your commitment to the Code of a Loving Heart guides you as you decide what to do next and how to do it. You'll know you are getting complete when you start to feel a sense of liberation and when you feel your strength returning because you have made the courageous choice to live as a strong, confident warrior of love.

Just remember a moment when you had finished a difficult project or achieved a milestone that you worked on for a long time—a time when you were bursting with excitement, enthusiasm, and pride. In these holy moments, you're loving yourself; you're looking through the eyes of your divine heart. You've forgotten about the past, and you're not focusing on the future. You are in the moment, standing in pure acknowledgment and filled with awe.

Completion allows you to be present with everything as it exists right now. It gives you superhero vision, because when you are complete you commit to no longer looking through the eyes of your wounded self, through the eyes of your past, through the eyes of fear. Instead, you turn the corner, stand in the present moment, and declare yourself complete. Standing in completion, you declare that you are not going to dip into the past or listen to the familiar voices of fear and limitation that you've heard so many times before. When you are complete, you repeatedly discover a moment of pure perfection—the present moment, which is where you will find your courageous warrior and be sourced by your courage and confidence rather than by your fear.

Last year at one of my advanced trainings for coaches, I was talking about completion, and I began to think about what I needed to get complete with. I'd been feeling so drained and exhausted at that time, like I needed chlorophyll shot directly into my veins, because I was completely out of energy, which was rare for me. When I made a list of all the things I was incomplete with, I saw that in order to find my juice again, I needed to let people know that I couldn't work on their projects and that my schedule wouldn't allow me to be in regular communication or return their e-mails or calls. The prospect of setting this boundary terrified me.

When I asked myself why I was so scared, I could see that I thought that if I said no to people, I would lose love, or I would miss a big opportunity, or my career would fall apart. I had the evidence to support this fear. When I had disappointed people in the past, they had been mad at me. So I was saying yes to people I didn't even know and to projects I didn't even want to do, whether it was writing a foreword for a book, being on yet another person's teleclass, or doing an Internet radio show with twenty listeners. I would say yes whenever somebody said, "I need you. You're the only one that can help me," even though my highly trained staff and coaches are probably better at this than I am by now. And I would say yes after they'd gone to everybody who told them no, because I felt guilty. Even when I was on vacation, I would schedule calls that I would take while lying on beautiful beaches—in the very environments I had picked so that I could "relax and let go" for a while. So vacations became work-cations where I just tricked myself into thinking I was resting and taking time off. I came to realize that I was a people pleaser, even though I never used to believe I was. Clearly, my past was dictating my present, and I was definitely going to become part of the walking dead if something didn't shift.

What I was doing wasn't working. I was finally at the point of exhaustion, and I could feel a new day dawning. I began to feel more committed to having a life than to giving all my energy away. Sitting down with my executive assistant, I made a list of the people with whom I'd need to lovingly establish new boundaries so that I would no longer feel so depleted. Saying no forced me to dip into a reservoir of courage that I didn't even know I had. Gathering my inner forces, I delivered my communications swiftly, clearly, and with love.

The outcome was dramatic. The next day I had more energy and more life inside of me than I had felt in years, because I didn't look to the past to see how I had handled overwhelm before and who I allowed myself to be. Instead, I looked through the eyes of the future that I wanted. I embraced being a cowardly people pleaser, decided to be complete with her, and stepped into my courageous warrior woman—free at last.

One of the most surprising things I learned in the process of becoming complete with the past was that what I really needed was self-love. Somebody who truly loves herself with her heart wide open would never give all her energy away. I saw that I needed to forgive myself for all the times I'd chosen to have work conversations instead of taking care of myself; the times I'd texted people in the middle of my son's tennis games; or the times I'd skipped dinner so that I could lead a teleclass. Forgiving myself would require a commitment to loving myself that I had not yet made. Mahatma Gandhi said it best: "The only devils in the world are those running around in our hearts. That is where the battle should be fought."

In order to open your heart and love yourself completely, you must become aware of the convergence of thoughts and feelings inside of you, especially the inner dialogue that you're listening to each day. You may not realize that you have thousands of self-criticizing, negative thoughts about yourself until you begin to tune in and listen. I can promise you, it's not always a pretty picture. If you are going to learn to love all of who you are, which I believe is one of the most difficult lessons for anyone to learn, you will find it in this pure, heartful space where you embrace the person you have been in all her glory and imperfections.

If you don't open your compassionate heart to yourself, you are guaranteed to be haunted by the cries from within and destined to set yourself up for the next round of self-sabotage. Your critical self-talk is a one-way ticket to a place of loneliness and isolation. People always tell me, "But I love part of myself," but they miss the point. Part of you isn't the whole of you. Self-love is about loving the whole, complete person that you are. So you have to discover where you're not loving yourself, knowing that every word that you say, every thought you think, even if you can't hear it or you're not listening, affects the way you feel about yourself and ultimately how much confidence you truly have.

For you to be in this place where you can choose to love, forgive, and be openhearted toward yourself, you must initiate a profound practice of awareness to heal and be complete with the wounded child within you. We have all been unconsciously conditioned to make ourselves wrong, criticize ourselves, beat ourselves up, and take the blame. To make up for all the years of wounding, and the years of love this part of you needed and didn't get, you need a daily practice that will heal the hurt that has closed your heart.

One of the most transformative practices I know involves ongoing attention to the child within. Self-love will ask you to bring a clear and kind awareness to this vulnerable part of yourself, where you can genuinely say "I'm sorry" for the times you second-guessed yourself, for the things you've done that make you feel bad, for the ways you've punished or deprived yourself, for the guilt you've carried for which you continue to shame yourself. In other words, you must open your heart to yourself over and over again.

Every time you catch yourself thinking something negative about yourself, or saying something that belittles or shames you, you must be humble enough and wise enough to know that it is just as hurtful as it would be if you were doing it to a young child over and over again. Imagine taking out a plastic bat or something that hurts and then, with every negative thought you think, hitting that child. It's a terrible image, but that's what you are doing to yourself when you are not complete with the past and refuse to forgive yourself. You must make time each day to apologize to yourself, to let the healing balm of honest remorse soothe your forgotten aches. This high level of respect will expedite your completion process and set the warrior free.

The point is not to beat yourself or make yourself wrong (perpetuating more of the same self-abuse), but to release yourself from the shackles of your own self-loathing.

Are you familiar with the Voice of Self-Loathing? It may sound something like this:

I don't deserve to be happy.

I'm unworthy.

I feel guilty.

I screwed up again.

They're going to hate me.

I'm a bitch.

I'm a phony.

I'm a fat slob.

I'm so disorganized.

I'm too sensitive.

I blew it again.

Nobody will ever want me.

And on and on and on . . .

To make yourself feel better and inflate your false confidence, you might have the tendency to highlight everything good about what you're doing, all the movement you're experiencing, all the progress you're making, and how far you've come. But the shadow of just looking at what's right is that everything else gets labeled as wrong or simply denied. You must forgive yourself for not listening to your own intuition, for not making your own choices, for not standing up for yourself. You must forgive yourself for the experiences you most regret. You must forgive yourself for being hard on yourself, making yourself wrong, making the mistakes you've made, saying yes when you meant no, allowing your boundaries to be crossed, being jealous, competitive, or envious, or keeping your mouth shut when you needed to speak up. The only antidote is to give yourself the love that you need, not to try to fix the past. You must remain humble enough to know that whatever is going on, your sacred child needs your attention—and not just some of the time but all of the time.

As you go through the process of unleashing enormous amounts of self-love, you may recognize with greater clarity all the things that have been obstructing it—your addictions, your cravings, and the different ways that you numb your emotions so you don't have to feel the depth of your self-loathing. You may use substances, working, staying busy, or being embroiled in your dramas (or other people's dramas if you don't have enough of your own) to avoid addressing what you really need, which is your own love, respect, attention, and deep sense of belonging. Your self-loathing robs you of joy, energy, and confidence, filling your body with tension, anxiety, grief, and an inability to receive—all of which diminish your courage. You may have become an expert at giving away to others the love that you so desperately need for yourself. But when you can be humble enough to take your inner child into your arms—to hold and nurture her, feeling deep in your heart how badly you want to protect her—you can give voice to your apologies for making her wrong, for not listening to her, and for the thousand times you've judged her.

One of my students, Lydia, shared that she felt she couldn't be complete with her past and love herself because she was still forty pounds overweight. She had struggled with her weight for most of her life and had tried everything—food plans, trainers, packaged foods, Weight Watchers, Jenny Craig, starving herself, fruit diets, meat diets, the Zone, and every other celebrity-endorsed plan. But she could never stick to anything, and nothing worked for long. Every year she would register for a new gym membership, but after just a few days she would crawl back in bed with her bowl of M&Ms, feeling miserable and hopeless. I suggested to her that her weight was really just a symptom of a deeper issue and asked her when she had decided that she hated her body. Lydia couldn't answer because she couldn't identify a time when weight hadn't been an issue. It was as if her body hatred had been evenly distributed over the past thirty-four years, and recalling a specific moment felt next to impossible.

I asked Lydia to go a little deeper, to take some deep breaths, and to get a little distance from the issue of her weight. I asked her to find some unrelated issue around her body that made her want to cover it up, disconnect, or beat herself up. After a few minutes of silence, Lydia dropped her head in shame and told me this story.

When she was thirteen years old, Lydia got pregnant for the first time. Scared and confused, she was relieved when she miscarried early enough in the pregnancy that she didn't have to suffer her family's shame. Twenty-one years later, Lydia was surprised to find out that she was pregnant again. She never wanted children with her husband, but she thought it would make him happy to have a child. In the face of his excitement, she felt ashamed that she didn't want the baby. She was so embarrassed and in pain about the way she felt that she hid it from everybody and pretended to be the happy, expectant mother. Although she experienced a few fleeting moments of joy while pregnant, when her daughter finally arrived, her first thought was "What am I going to do with her? I don't really want her."

Lydia was horrified by her own dark thoughts. She cried with shame, saying, "I can never forgive myself for having these feelings." Recounting the memory, she realized that it was at that time that her body became her enemy. And then she remembered more vividly how frivolous and careless she had been with boys as a child, allowing them to cross her boundaries and do things to her that resulted in her getting pregnant that first time, before she was anywhere near ready for it. I asked Lydia to write a forgiveness letter to the scared, young part of her.

Dear beautiful, sweet, loving child,

From the deepest part of my heart, I am sorry that I hurt and mistreated you. I am sorry for not listening to you and for not holding you close to me when you were so afraid and lonely. I am sorry to have abandoned you so early in life and for all of the emotional and physical toxins that I allowed into your perfect body, soul, and spirit. You asked

me to protect you and to trust that God would always be there, and I
turned away from you because of my own beliefs and fears.

My love, I feel awful for the way that I let boys and men treat
your body. You are a divine angel, and I allowed it to be used like an
amusement park. I am sorry that because of this, I allowed us to be
pregnant and always wished that I hadn't.

I'm sorry that I gave up on you, on God, and on myself.

I am sorry for ignoring you when you would shout out loud to try
and stop me from making a choice that didn't serve us. It was like I was
going through life with earplugs and a blindfold. I was so conflicted and
confused. I thought I had sinned, and yet I thought there was no God.
So I gave up and decided that it doesn't matter what I do or how I treat
myself. I am sorry for laughing at you, for making fun of you, for not
making you feel safe and loved. I want you to know now that it does
matter, that you matter, that we matter, and that we can make a positive
and loving difference.

I am writing to you today to tell you how sorry I am and ask that
you please forgive me. Being the divine soul that you are, I ask for this
forgiveness from a place of love and humility.

I love you. Please forgive me. Thank you, blessed one.

Lydia

When Lydia finished reading her letter out loud, she looked
like she had instantly dropped twenty pounds. After she opened
up her heart to the part of her that held the wounds of her past, as
amazing as it always is to me, she was able to commit to dropping
her extra weight. But more important, she suddenly felt a deep
and overwhelming love for her daughter, whom she'd always kept

at arm's length. She could hug her child like she'd never hugged her before and could look into her eyes with the pure knowing that she had no malice in her heart. She went for walks with her and had meaningful conversations that previously would have gone unspoken. Now Lydia was filled with so much confidence about being a loving and attentive mother and having the courage to let go of the past that she could stand as a powerful warrior mother with a newfound joy.

I asked others in my group of students to write forgiveness letters to the child inside them, apologizing for ignoring them and discounting their value.

Renata was working on her perfectionism so that she could find the courage to become visible, to be in the limelight, and to "take up a little space." Here is what she had to say to her inner child.

Dear Little One,

It's been a long half a century. You've spent so much time and energy just trying to measure up. I am so incredibly sorry that I have abandoned you and left you feeling like you simply weren't good enough . . . didn't matter . . . had nothing profound to contribute . . . weren't significant enough to take up any real space in the world. I am so sorry I have encouraged you to please, perform, and prove your life away—to be the perfect little girl. I can see your exhaustion. I can feel your desire to simply "be" rather than "do."

I am so sorry, honey, that I have not reminded you of your value every single day. I'm sorry that I haven't assured you that you are priceless just as you are! "Nothing you need to add, nothing that needs to be taken away." How many times have you heard that message? But I have never allowed it to really land in your heart.

I am so deeply sorry for turning my back on your woundedness. I have minimized, dismissed, disowned, and discredited your pain. I have not acknowledged your needs, wants, or desires. I have silenced you mercilessly, lest any kind of "authentic truth" escape your lips and let people know how much you and I are hurting.

I am so sorry for the facade. I am so sorry for the lack of compassion and empathy I have shown you. I have beaten you down when you made a mistake. I have crushed your spirit if you asked a "stupid" question. I have shamed you for being human. I have shamed you for having needs. I have shamed you for being anything less than profound in every space of your life. Please forgive me. I am so sorry.

You have worked so hard to please me. I have been heartless and cruel in my treatment of you. I have failed to hear your pleas for help. I have allowed you to suffer and then blamed you for crying. I have taken the best you had to offer and picked it apart . . . ruthlessly.

You deserve so much more than this. You are such a magnificent and loving heart. You have brought so much light to the world already! It is my solemn intention that from now on, you get to make mistakes. You get to cry. You get to be sad. You get to be adequate, maybe even mediocre if that is your goal for the day! I give you permission to fall short, fall down, say when you are hurt, and ask for the love and support you need and deserve.

I promise to acknowledge you from now on. I promise to make room for your voice. When I wake up in the morning, I will take five minutes and invite you to come out from behind the "tree of strength." I will listen for your beautiful wisdom. I will make every effort to honor your

*tenderness with the kindness and compassion you so rightly deserve as I
make my way through the day.*

*Yes, you deserve it! You really do deserve it! And if I slip up, please
be unyielding in your attempts to remind me. I hereby revoke my self-
appointed right to silence you.*

*I want to hear you singing now, singing because you know you
deserve to be heard! We will be able to go out with our arms wide open
and a big smile on our face, feeling complete with our past and proud of
all of who we are.*

Love,

Renata

Evelyn had just been through another bad breakup and was
experiencing a lot of emotional pain, blaming herself for all the
mistakes she had made and for what now looked like a foolish
choice—to get involved with a man that she didn't really know.

Dear perfect, sweet, loving little girl,

*Words will never express how sorry I am that I've deserted you,
abandoned you, and beat you up for years. You are so sweet and
innocent, and yet I made you pay for all the things that happened to
me in life that didn't go my way or that I had no control over. You've
suffered for things that had no relation to you and took on the struggles
and pain of others around you when no small child should ever be made
to do that. I made you responsible for my parents' discord and for all the
mistakes I made because I didn't listen to you when you were screaming
at me what to do. I locked you in a closet and neglected you, and I am
so, so, sorry; for you have been my dearest friend and love and I did not*

reciprocate. Please, please forgive me, as I promise to be there for you always and to listen closely to what you need from me—and then to give it to you without question.

   I love you and I bless you. I'm so excited to clear the slate and to start a new life with you. I know that together we will have the courage now to move powerfully forward.

Love,

Evelyn

After each person read her letter out loud, it was clear that the sincerity of the apologies opened their hearts and allowed them to feel the deep love that exists inside. The words "I'm sorry" were the key to opening the door to real forgiveness. "I'm sorry, I love you, please forgive me." And with that, an explosion of love came through everyone's hearts. When I asked people what they would say to themselves every day to replace any negative chatter, here's what they shared:

Love yourself for all the good that you bring to the world.

Love yourself for working so hard to be a better person.

Love yourself for all the gifts that you bring.

Love yourself for all the things that you have gotten right.

Love yourself, for there is only one person in the world like you.

Love yourself for the courage and the confidence it takes to do your inner work.

Love yourself for all the ways you take care of yourself.

Be proud of what you've done, not what you haven't done.

Be unconditionally accepting of yourself.

When you are filled with self-love, you have the courage to tackle your deepest fears and the confidence to do whatever it will take to succeed at your tasks. When you are filled with self-love, you open up to a rightness about yourself that comes not from the circumstances of your outer world, not from the achievements and accolades of your ego, but from the very center of your being. You gain the ability to look at yourself through divine eyes, seeing the perfection in all parts of yourself, where everything comes easy, where everything just works out. I am talking about a holy perfection, about knowing and being so connected to the Divine that you understand there is a design that is helping you evolve into a divine warrior whose love for self and others knows no bounds.

THE LOVING HEART PROCESS

Light a candle, open your journal, take a slow, deep breath, and open up to a whole new level of loving honesty.

1. **Eavesdropping on your negative self-talk:** Tune in to your inner dialogue to identify the negative chatter about yourself. Make a list of what the Voice of Self-Loathing is saying to you about yourself. What do you criticize yourself for? What do you make wrong about yourself?

2. **The cost of self-loathing:** Make a list of the cost and the consequences of listening to this internal dialogue. How does it rob you of your courage and your confidence?

3. **The pure power of atonement:** Write a letter of deep apology to the wounded child inside of you. Tell her the specific things you are sorry for doing or saying to her. Let the words "I'm sorry" guide you.

4. **Daily doses of loving connection:** Begin a daily practice of visiting your wounded inner child, taking time to acknowledge her and to say "I'm sorry" if she was ignored or hurt in some way during the day.

5. **Self-talk that heals:** Make a list of the positive things you can say to yourself every day to replace the negative chatter and to boost your courage, confidence, and self-love.

6. **Your Completion List:** Make a Completion List of anything you need to handle or address in order to be complete with your past.

7. **Taking action to free your heart:** Based on your Completion List, take the necessary actions to be done with the past and free to be the courageous, confident force that you are.

Courage Activator

Find three people you need to make amends with, and, with a heart-opening call or e-mail, say you're sorry and send them your love. Making amends when you're scared can give you more courage than you ever imagined.

Confidence Builder

Look at any projects you're involved in where you know you need to draw a line in the sand. Communicate with one of the people associated with at least one of the projects to let him or her know that you won't be doing it right now. This will give you the confidence to know that you can tell your authentic truth.

Courage and Confidence Bonus

Make a list of seven amends you've made in the past to people you have hurt in some way.

The Code of
Inspired Vision

Imagine waking up each morning with an excitement and passion you haven't felt in years. Imagine going through each day enjoying every moment, feeling purposeful and fulfilled. Imagine having all the courage and confidence you need to conquer your world.

The warrior of love lights up the room everywhere she goes. Her eyes are beaming with love, with compassion, with the radiance of knowing that life is a profound gift. She knows that she has a divine imprint. And from that imprint, the purpose and plan for her life emerge. Her courage and confidence come from this knowing. Her strength reveals the most beautiful and vulnerable parts of herself. She is excited and happy to be a part of this universe. She is committed to being the best that she can possibly be, and her vision is one that is uniquely her own.

The courageous warrior never forgets that there is boldness, genius, power, and magic in doing whatever it is she dreams of. With her beautiful, clear vision, she looks directly into the heart of life, loving it with an intensity that transforms. She loves every cell in her body deeply, loves every bit of human consciousness profoundly, regards every bit of history with awe, accepts every bit of the world and everyone in it with deep appreciation. She has the capacity to open her arms wide to all that is. The beaming force that comes through her is a union of imagination and creativity. She is tapped into the divine force, the beautiful source that speaks through her, that can see a future greater than what her human eyes can see. It is with her imagination that she opens up and looks around the world with new eyes, the eyes of the courageous, confident warrior of love. She knows that every bit of creativity is ultimately coming through the mind of God. She has no need to be the sole proprietor of the business of living, preferring instead to be in a high-powered partnership with the creative force of the universe. This is who we are. This is who you are. This is the warrior of love.

An inspired vision will always move you forward from where you are today. When you trust the universe, you get to play in the magical world of God's plan. So now is the time for you to use your courage and confidence to unleash your unbridled imagination. It is time to allow your vision to come through you. A vision is more than a list written out on the pages of your journal that describes your goals for the next two to five years. And it's even more than the future you proclaim that you want when talking to your best friends or your colleagues. All of those things are incredibly important and valuable, each in its own way. But what is crucial to understand is that an inspired vision is a dynamic, living force with the power to move you from where you are today to where your heart wants you to be.

This is saying a lot, because it's not easy to get most of us to move. Inspired vision can imaginatively draw your attention away from the past and get you excited about living right now. It has the power to awaken you from the trance induced by repetitively thinking about old fears, hurts, and regrets and put you in the presence of why you are here.

To experience the thrill of your highest expression and transcend the life you are living right now, you will have to commit to an inspired vision that demands you be the biggest, best "you" that you can possibly be. When you are deeply rooted in a clear, strong, and compelling vision, you will experience a level of joy and celebration that you probably haven't felt in years. And you will absolutely have the courage and confidence you need to live into your vision. I know this beyond the shadow of a doubt, because I have seen miracle after miracle happen when passionate women make commitments and keep them. When we get serious about not allowing familiar excuses and obstacles to keep us from living our highest purpose, settling for fear and low self-confidence is no longer an option.

A strong, clear vision holds the power to transcend your current reality, bypassing the day-to-day challenges that might be keeping you stuck where you are. An inspired or divine vision acts as a force that lifts you out of the drama and predictability of daily life and supports you in making extraordinary choices.

These new choices will unlock your passion. And vision and passion are two sides of the same coin. One does not exist without the other. Once you begin to heed the call of your vision, tired old voices like cynicism and resignation fade away, overwhelmed by the inner choir of hope, enthusiasm, optimism, and passion.

Vision lifts you up. It makes you smile a secret smile because you know that you have something very special to share. If you want to connect deeply with your warrior sisters around the world, let us know what you're passionate about and what matters to you by sharing your vision. The bar of possibility is raised for everyone when you pull back the curtain and make your dreams visible to all. I will assert that one of the reasons you, as a visionary warrior, are here is to open our collective eyes to things we have never considered before.

To follow the path of inspired vision, you must allow yourself to be intuitively pulled toward something other than what you know right now or what you can see. When you are humble enough to be used as a messenger and an instrument of the Divine, it is easy to see that your vision chooses you and that you have the choice of whether to honor it.

I love looking into the eyes of someone who is inspired by a vision greater than herself. In the reflecting pool of her eyes, I see new worlds glistening back at me. One night a girlfriend of mine invited me to go to dinner with someone I didn't know very well—the mother of one of my son's friends. The three of us slipped quietly into a booth at one of our favorite restaurants. Margie, the mother of my son's friend, was sitting across from me. Her smile excited me and brought a smile to my face. I could see that she was someone who was lit up by something. We started talking and getting to know each other when Margie asked me how I came to write a book and how I became who I am as a teacher. Then she told me her own inspiring story.

From a very young age Margie was fascinated and curious about the military. She'd never met anyone in the military and didn't even know anyone who knew anyone in the military. Yet when they studied the military in school, Margie became intrigued and wanted to learn more about how it worked and what kinds of people would go into it, particularly in a time of war. Even as a young girl, she felt a yearning deep in her heart to touch the lives of those young men and women who would sign up to fight for our country. As she began to tell me her story, her eyes twinkled even brighter, and I could feel the passion coming through her and the excitement in every word she uttered. She talked about how when she trained as a psychotherapist, she kept imagining herself helping these people, even though she had no idea how she would do it.

She told me about her first contract with the military, a five-week job at a summer school at a military base in Germany. She was shocked by the perks of her position—a two-bedroom apartment, a per diem, and a BMW at her disposal. She felt like a princess but was also unsettled by the waste of resources and taxpayer dollars. The following summer, she worked at a summer camp in Italy for the children of deployed soldiers.

Next she got a six-week contract as a counselor at a counseling center on a military base in San Diego. The counseling center was extremely unpopular on the base because it was where people were sent when they were mandated to get counseling, and anything that happened there became part of their permanent record. With little to do, Margie was asked to reorganize the supply room, inventory office supplies, and clean out storage cabinets. A few days before her contract was set to expire, Margie tiptoed out onto the base to meet the people she had come there so eager to serve. Some of the new friends she made invited her to run a group for their division, helping the drill instructors to manage their stress. Margie was delighted and excited to be able to make a difference. Her contract was extended, and she developed an extremely successful and effective program. Word spread on the base, and she began to offer groups to more divisions. The thrill only increased each day as she headed to work. The soldiers kept requesting her services, and she stayed at the base for over a year.

Unfortunately, the higher-ups did not share the soldiers' enthusiasm, and one day Margie was handed a slip stating that she had thirty minutes to get off the base. Although she didn't get an explanation, she told me she thought she was dismissed for failing to document her work, neglecting the proper paperwork, and defying military protocols.

But now, entirely absorbed by her vision, she would let nothing stop her. She started to consult with counselors inside the military mental-health system. She went to Washington, D.C., to lobby about the importance of preventative military mental-health care. Suddenly, the group of political representatives with whom she had toured through Israel a few years earlier became an invaluable network for her lobbying efforts. (I remember seeing this post on her Facebook page: "I'm going to D.C. I have back-to-back meetings with congressmen and congresswomen. I'm taking three suits, six pairs of shoes, and a black lacy bra because I'm willing to do anything to get their attention.")

After our dinner, Margie called me often. I had suggested to her that she write her story and then publish it as a book. Even though Margie told me she couldn't write and she wouldn't know how to begin, she stepped through her fear and allowed her courage and her divine vision to guide her. She was a warrior, and nothing was going to stop her now. She decided not to wait for people to come to her, so she e-mailed her book proposal to more than sixty publishers and received six responses by the next morning. As she stepped into her vision more and more, the universe met her. Of course, she encountered stumbling blocks along the way. People questioned her credentials, since she had only a master's degree and not a Ph.D., and then questioned her credibility, since she was a civilian and not a member of the military. But she would not be swayed in her commitment to her divine vision.

When I asked her why she hadn't just returned to her successful private practice when she was dismissed from the base, what it was that kept her going, she told me she couldn't look at herself in the mirror at night if she wasn't helping these people. She knew that the men and women who vowed to protect all of us and our freedom were being robbed of the tools and the support they needed to take on their vital mission.

Margie told me she could remember the day when what she had first thought was a burden of responsibility turned into a divine gift. During a counseling session with a forty-six-year-old drill instructor, he broke down and began crying, putting his head in his hands. "You have to help us," he said. "You can't stop." And she doesn't. Any time she begins to falter—wondering, "What's in this for me? Why am I doing this?"—she inevitably gets a call from a Marine needing her support, a counselor trying to change a life in a broken system, a reporter writing an article, or a senator's aide who wants to learn more.

Today when I talk to Margie, I continue to get inspired by her vision. I've watched the world line up around her to support her in doing what only a year ago looked to her like an impossible task.

I don't think the power of commitment has ever been illuminated any better than it was by W. H. Murray:

Until one is committed there is hesitancy, the chance to draw back, always ineffectiveness. Concerning all acts of initiative (and creation), there is one elementary truth, the ignorance of which kills countless ideas and splendid plans: that the moment one definitely commits oneself, then Providence moves too. All sorts of things occur to help one that would never otherwise have occurred. A whole stream of events issue from the decision, raising in one's favor all manner of unforeseen incidents and meetings and material assistance, which no person could have dreamt would come their way. Whatever you can do, or you can dream, begin it. Boldness has genius, power and magic in it.

When someone is present to their vision, we can feel it in our body. Why the universe lines up—offering all manner of re-sources, connections, and support—is because it holds a certain vibration that draws us to it. We're inspired by it. We want to help. We know it's for something greater than we may be able to grasp through ordinary consciousness.

Everybody's vision is unique, and at different times in their lives their vision changes. It may be smaller and more personal for a while, and then it may grow larger, expanding outward to the world. When someone has been trying to have a baby and finally gets pregnant and has so much joy in her heart, you want to give her a hug and wish her well. Or when someone finally takes a risk and steps into a new job, you can feel her tremendous desire to be a great employee and to make a difference. Or when someone finally takes on her health and commits to losing sixty pounds, you cheer her on as you watch her struggle with determination because she wants to show her kids she can do it. You are so inspired that you want to be on their team.

Another one of my inspiring girlfriends came to spend Thanksgiving weekend with me. We both seemed to be at the same stage, having accomplished a great deal in the outer world but really needing something to pep us up, a new vision. We'd had many visions and fulfilled so many of them. I could tell that Cynthia, who is very charismatic and alive, was missing something. Her inner fire had gone out, the spark in her eyes was missing, and she described a vague dissatisfaction with her life. The more we talked, the more bored she got, eventually lying down on the couch and pulling a blanket over her.

Just then, my friend Vivian Glyck, another great warrior and the founder of the Just Like My Child Foundation, came by to say hello and visit with us. As we talked about the school my son was building in Uganda for his bar mitzvah project, Cynthia's eyes popped open. She sat straight up on the couch and threw off the blanket. She went from dead as a doornail to completely lit up and inspired in two seconds flat. She said, "That's it!"—and we spent the rest of the weekend planning how she could turn her fiftieth birthday party into a fund-raiser for building schools in Africa. Suddenly, Cynthia could see possibilities that she hadn't seen before. The network of transformational leaders and teachers with whom she worked was instantly transformed into a network of support for giving. She realized she had contacts everywhere, and they were happy to partner with her.

Two years earlier, Cynthia had been invited by a friend to the Rural African Women's Conference. Although she didn't know why, and although it didn't make sense in her head, her heart told her she had to go. She rearranged her schedule and made the trip, emerging from the event inspired to support African women and their children in their effort to move out of poverty through education. But she had no idea how to do it. Now, two years later, she was taking action, and her birthday party fund-raiser brought in eighty thousand dollars.

Cynthia felt excited about living her purpose, but she still had to run a full-time business. There was a part of her that said, "I would love to do this full-time," but that voice was met immediately with a quick retort: "How could you do that? You're single. You need to make money." She couldn't see how to turn her calling into her career, so she stuck with her business. She would try from time to time to muster up the courage to take the leap, but something would always intervene, like an unexpected expense or the economy taking a steep downturn. Even when she got re-inspired and momentarily excited by working on her foundation, Cynthia stayed in the comfort zone of her successful business, thinking to herself, "Who is going to pay me money to teach others to give? Who is going to support causes in this economy?"

Cynthia traveled to Africa again, to see the results of the work her birthday donations had funded, and she came home fully connected to her vision—completely inspired, excited, joyful, and strong in the knowledge that her work in Africa is her calling. Every child she met in Africa helped her to see that she needed to be the brightest and highest expression of herself; she needed to step more fully into her vision. If she didn't step up and step in, who would?

When she returned from Africa, it was time for her to sell her next round of corporate coaching programs. She knew that, but she experienced tremendous resistance. She would call me and tell me how badly she didn't want to do it but that another side of her was saying, "You have to!" As she sat down at her desk each day to run her business, she felt stuck, bored, uninspired, and frustrated. But she didn't believe she had any alternative. "I can't just quit my business," she told herself. "How would it work?"

A quiet, small voice inside of her nudged her, saying, "Maybe this is the time. Why don't you do your foundation full-time?" But Cynthia's fear of how she would survive stifled and silenced the voice over and over again. One night, Cynthia forced herself to stay up and write the marketing copy for her new program—a task that she'd been avoiding. Then, after hours of work, and completing copy that she felt good about, her computer crashed and she lost every bit of text that she had just written. After she had knuckled her way through this task, forcing herself to do it, she could hardly believe that she was looking at a blank computer screen. She ended up going to sleep completely frustrated.

Cynthia awoke at three in the morning. She could feel anxiety coursing through her body. She heard that quiet voice again: "Cynthia, why don't you just do your foundation full-time?" This time, exhausted, Cynthia didn't fight back. She didn't argue. She gave it the space to just be there. Later that morning, when she went to work out, the voice returned, and again, she let it be there. The more she listened to the voice, the more she started feeling that this was a possibility. Something started changing and shifting inside of her. She could feel her vision pulling her, and she couldn't fight it anymore. She couldn't say no.

When Cynthia made the decision to make her foundation her full-time job, in the holy moment when she realized she just couldn't put it off any longer, she moved into action. She called her assistant, her marketing partner, and her business partner and told them to shut the business down. Shocked by the decisiveness of her courage and the clarity of her confidence when she wasn't listening to the Voice of Fear, she finally felt peace—total peace.

Cynthia made the commitment to call three people a day to engage them in support of her next fund-raising campaign. After her second call, she unexpectedly found a sponsor for her entire campaign. At that moment, Cynthia knew she was provided for. She knew that God would provide for all of her needs if she had the courage to be a full Yes. In her full, courageous Yes, she stepped into a place of joyous creation. No longer did she have to struggle, agonize, try, or make it work. In her full Yes, Cynthia attracted the people and the resources she needed for her divine vision. And the process hasn't stopped.

Because Cynthia stood firmly in the shoes of her brave, courageous warrior of love—because of her love for African children, for humanity, and for the universe itself—and because she remained committed to her divine vision, Cynthia's foundation has funded twenty-two primary schools, one secondary classroom, and two dormitories; 5,169 people have clean water, 7,169 have access to health care, 225 adults have received income training, and 66 women have earned scholarships. The world is truly a different place. And on top of it all, Cynthia met the love of her life.

If Margie or Cynthia had chosen to listen to the Voice of Fear, they both would most likely have lived nice lives, but they would be missing the passion and the purpose that fuel not only them and those around them, but all of the people they are helping around the world. Our inspired vision needs to be inspiring enough to trump the mind, the ego, and the fears that naturally pop up. We must distinguish those voices as voices of the past so that we continue to believe in our vision and not our limitations.

I have seen a great many people over the years get clear on their vision, start to work toward it for a few months, and then get distracted or dissatisfied when things aren't going exactly as they think they should. So they move on. They do something else. They start down the path of a new vision. The fact that a vision is divine doesn't mean it's going to be easy. It takes ups and downs, twists and turns, but it's a beautiful ride if we stay in the seat as a divine messenger and allow ourselves to be used for a purpose.

And it's essential that we allow ourselves to open up over and over again to where the universe wants to guide us. It's not our job to assess the merit of our vision or judge its importance. It is our job to receive the vision and act upon it.

I've written several times about the day I got struck with my divine vision. I was sitting in front of the Aventura Mall in North Miami Beach, where I owned a clothing store named Mile High. After coming out of my fourth drug-treatment center, I was confused and bored with life. I couldn't imagine how I was going to live without drugs or something to make myself feel better. But on this day, all of a sudden at a stop light, I got emotionally choked up when I realized that I could make a difference for other people who had gone through the same kinds of issues that I had gone through. It wasn't just a little thought. It was like a bolt of lightning, a blast of fireworks going off inside me. "Wow! I could write a book! I have something to share!"

Suddenly the whole world that I thought I was glued to— fashion, living in Florida, going to twelve-step meetings every day—melted away, and a spark lit inside me that has rarely left me since. I started looking into schools and what I wanted to study. I was clear after taking many standard psychology classes that I wanted to go down a more inspiring path of learning. There was a different kind of learning happening, a field that merged psychology and consciousness studies, and the only place I could get a degree in it was John F. Kennedy University, in Orinda, California. I told my business partner that I wanted to sell the store. I sold all of my belongings, moved to northern California, and took every consciousness course, transpersonal psychology course, and writing course the university offered. I wrote and wrote. I learned new tools and techniques. And my vision kept getting bigger and more beautiful.

I almost got detoured when I married and got pregnant with my son, Beau, but a year later I got back on track and wrote my first bestselling book, *The Dark Side of the Light Chasers: Reclaiming Your Power, Creativity, Brilliance, and Dreams.* Everything lined up. My sister, who was close to Deepak Chopra, introduced my work to him, and I quickly became a part of the Chopra Center team that was doing the emotional wholeness work that I seemed to be naturally gifted to do. After starting a speaking tour, I got invited to do three Oprah Winfrey shows, which skyrocketed my book to number one on the *New York Times* bestseller list.

When my second divine vision arrived, which was to write a book called *Spiritual Divorce,* I wanted to hide my head under the blanket, because what I really wanted was to write a book called "How to Kill My Husband and Get Away with It." (And just to let you know, writing *Spiritual Divorce* got me over the other title, and I have been extremely blessed, which no doubt the universe had a lot to do with, to have the best ex-husband and father of my child that one could wish for.) Since I was so committed to everyone having the opportunity to understand the underbelly of humanity—which is what took me to the whole next level of my own mental health and emotional freedom—I started the Ford Institute for Transformational Training in order to teach coaches, executives, and businesspeople all over the world how to transform their own lives and support others in transforming theirs. I've written six more books since then, and I produced a documentary called *The Shadow Effect*.

Each time I stand up and give a lecture in front of people who have no idea how our emotional pain affects our entire lives and blinds us to our divine vision, the light sparkles in my eyes, my smile extends past my body, my heart opens wider than I ever thought it could, and I thank God that I get to be used for a greater cause. Even though many times it hasn't been easy and I haven't wanted to do it, even though I've wanted someone else to have my vision because mine never stops making demands on me, the divinely inspired voice from above comes to me and whispers in my ear, "It's time to work on this" or "It's time to write about this" or "It's time to birth a new conversation in the world." And I take it one step at a time. I often don't know what's coming. But I'm very clear about this: I'm much more committed to God's will than to my will. When my audiences ask, "How do you do this?" I say, "I'm a great order taker. I listen well. I do what they say." Who are "they"? I don't really know. But they've been my guides and my source, turning me from weak, scared, and cowardly to bold, courageous, and confident.

Just like me, you have a vision right now. It may not be one that you recognize yet. It may live deep within you, stirring quietly below the surface. But it will see the light of day. Because, just like the sun obscured by clouds or by the fall of night, it is always there, waiting for you to bask in its golden light. Your vision is a precious gift from the Divine.

If you are not yet in the presence of your vision, start with what you love. Anything that inspires you, excites you, and motivates you in your life is sparked by the Divine. There is nothing you truly desire that you can't do. You can use your vision to become courageous, confident, and fearless, each day praying to see how you can be used by these qualities. See yourself each morning and night as being able to forge ahead powerfully, being able to stand boldly. See that you are a vision of your own strength, your own power, your own courage, and your own confidence. Don't try to make it come, because it's already there.

Once you recognize the vision, you must allow yourself to clearly distinguish what it feels like and allow yourself to feel it fully. If the vision makes you feel proud, you have to be able to feel that pride all the way down in your cells. If your vision makes you come alive, you have to allow that feeling of aliveness to permeate your whole life.

You must see your vision, believe your vision, feel your vision, and express it passionately out in the world. When you are in the presence of your vision, your inner world shifts. And it is only when your inner world shifts that your outer world can line up and guide you. The next right actions will be revealed to you, and the universe will move heaven and earth to support you in your vision.

To harness the power of an inspired and divine vision, you must keep it in your mind's eye each day. You must get up in the morning and ask, "What is in my highest and best interest that will allow me to serve myself and the world?" At night before you go to sleep, affirm your vision again, like a prayer to the universe. Allow it to grow with the help of your radiant focus and attention, because as it is imprinted on your conscious mind, it will continue to guide you and bring forth all those who are designed to support you in your vision. That's why people who step fully into their vision are always shocked: they see it, they feel it, they know it can exist *even when they don't know how*. This is where trust and faith are your partners in delivering your vision to the world.

You are a courageous warrior of love, with unique gifts to offer the world. The Divine gave these gifts to you, and now is the time for you to deliver them. There is nobody in the world like you, and you hold a source of power that nobody else in the world has. The light that will come forth from within you will help you heal yourself and all those who come into your presence. The world needs you. And your vision offers a path for spreading that courageous light far and wide.

THE INSPIRED VISION PROCESS

Find one of your favorite places to write, and take a few moments to breathe and relax. Once you feel in touch with yourself, pick up your pen and embark on this exciting and inspiring journaling exercise.

1. **Your divine purpose:** Ask the Divine to show you how it wants to use you for the good of all. Even if you think you already know what this is, allow yourself to see and know your purpose through the eyes of your warrior.

2. **Calling on the power of your imagination**: Unleash your imagination and creativity. Allow yourself to see a vision of your future in which you're passionately living your purpose and exuding profound courage and confidence.

3. **Your divine resources**: Make a list of the actions you would take, the people you would surround yourself with, and the resources you would need to move forward with your divine vision.

4. **Acknowledging your fear**: Make a list of the fears you have about living your divine vision. Give voice to the fear, and as you make the list, send love to this part of yourself.

5. **Being in the presence of your vision**: Put in place a simple practice or activity that keeps you in the presence of your divine vision every day.

Courage Activator

Take a risk by doing something that you've been scared to do or about which you've said, "I will never do that" because you're so fearful. Color your hair, take a balloon ride, jump out of a plane (please don't get hurt), sing karaoke. Allow your fearless self to come out this week and support you in activating all of your inner courage.

Confidence Builder

Make a list of why the world needs you as a courageous warrior and how you will use your divine strength and power in the future. Share your list with five people you feel safe and comfortable with.

Courage and Confidence Bonus

Make a list of five times when you helped somebody or were of service to the world.

The Code of
Supreme Beauty

It was December 1972. After flashing my fake ID, I slid into the hippest club in New York City. The music was blasting as my friends and I stepped onto the dance floor to revel in the number one hit:

I am woman, hear me roar
In numbers too big to ignore
And I know too much to go back an' pretend
'cause I've heard it all before
And I've been down there on the floor
No one's ever gonna keep me down again

Oh yes I am wise
But it's wisdom born of pain

Yes, I've paid the price
But look how much I gained
If I have to
I can do anything
I am strong (strong)
I am invincible (invincible)
I am woman

I could feel my body filling up with power, strength, and excitement. The thrill of each word vibrated through my body. All around, hundreds of people were dancing, and women were singing at the top of their lungs, "I am woman, hear me roar." I was thinking, "Yes! Yes! Yes!" I felt so great that night. I was wearing one of my favorite outfits—purple spandex pants, a strapless sequined multicolored top, and strapless sandals covered in rhinestones. (I promise you, that was in style back then.) I had spent hours that day in a salon turning my long straight hair into the latest style of permed hair. My skin was dark brown from the sun, and I was a Diana Ross lookalike. Now singing along with Helen Reddy—"I can do anything! I am strong. I am invincible. I am woman!"—I felt absolutely on top of the world.

I knew this could be true for every other woman, but I still had hesitation about myself. It scared me to think that I could do anything, because so many times I had tried and failed. But the idea of feeling that courageous power inside me each day was thrilling beyond measure. There was nothing I wanted more than to be confident in who I was. Even back then, I knew that I would have to give up playing small and dwelling in any internal conversations that made me feel "less than." I went back to my friend's apartment that night thinking about some of the girls I went to school with and women I had met along the way whom I was drawn to, who emanated their own kind of power and light. As I was dozing off, I could picture my high school friend Mary.

When Mary and I would come home from school, she would put on her ballet shoes, rise up on her toes, and do the most graceful and elegant pirouettes. She walked with elegance. Her posture was perfect. Her attitude was fun. She was always laughing, smiling, and twirling around. Although I never told her, I was very jealous about how good she seemed to feel about herself. She was a master at making light of her mistakes and moving on after any rejection. I wanted that kind of confidence and inner peace, and I went to sleep that night (after an evening of disco bliss) completely committed to finding out how to get it.

I woke up the next day wondering what kind of person felt confident, courageous, and strong enough to get up every morning and jump for joy, knowing they can do anything. While making myself breakfast, I started thinking back to something that happened one day at my fourth drug treatment center. I walked into a room for one of the regular group meetings and there was an overly made-up woman standing there who perkily introduced herself as Sandy. She said she wanted us to get to know her, although I couldn't imagine why, and she began rattling off details about herself I wasn't sure I even wanted to know: "I grew up in a small town with a really loving family. I worked hard in school so I would get a full scholarship to the best college in the state. I graduated from college with honors." "Uh-oh," I thought.

As I settled deeper into my seat, trying to find something in what she shared that interested me, she continued on: "I've been married for thirteen years, and I have a fabulous relationship with my husband. I pride myself now on being a really great wife, mother, sister, daughter, and friend." I listened to her rattle on about how great she was. I wanted to stand up and yell, "Well, good for you, lady!" I thought I would run out of there screaming if I had to listen for one more minute. *What a conceited bitch!* While my litany of judgments continued, Sandy was looking around the room, trying to make eye contact with as many of us as she could. I was proud of how cold and icy my stare was when her eyes met mine. Then she said something I'll never forget: "This is a lecture on self-love. This is how we talk about ourselves when we love who we are."

I swear, my mouth fell to the floor, because I thought the topic of the lecture was "How Full of Myself I Can Be." But if that was what self-love sounded like, I certainly had never heard it. It was like an entirely new language that I had no idea how to speak. Unknowingly, I was practicing self-hate. I would never say nice things about myself that way because God forbid somebody should find out the truth. I figured people wouldn't believe me, they'd hate me, they'd be jealous of me, or they would just judge me the way I had judged Sandy. Shame filled my body. People would undoubtedly find out the truth—that I was not such a good person, that I was really a phony.

What I didn't understand at the time is that we are a constellation of *everything*, that every quality that exists in the universe exists inside of us—the dark and the light, the bad and the good, the selfish and the selfless. When I began to really understand this I was shocked, because I had focused only on the negative qualities that I had, never on the positive. When I realized that I contained all the positive qualities, too, I was filled with hope and optimism. Images of who I could be in the world put a glowing sparkle in my eyes.

Rilke wrote that "perhaps all the dragons of our lives are princesses who are only waiting to see us once, beautiful and brave. Perhaps everything terrible is, in its deepest being, something that needs our love." I already had a lot of evidence that I was selfish, incompetent, and stupid, but now I knew that I was the polar opposite as well. I was also a magnificent and brilliant woman whose heart was as wide as the world.

Tell me, could there be anything as fantastic as that being your truth, too? Breathe this in: *You are a hot, sexy, delicious woman of the world whose job as a courageous warrior is to show all of your extraordinary, goddess-like self and to fill up your reservoir with so much love that you can be rejected by 99 percent of the world and still feel great about yourself.*

It is time to recognize your gifts and talents, to appreciate and honor all that you do well. It is time to search out your uniqueness, applaud and acknowledge yourself, and let your own light shine. I know that for many it's embarrassing to think you're great, beautiful, kind, loving, or smart. It's especially embarrassing to say it out loud. Maybe you were told not to be cocky or conceited. Maybe you even believe that downplaying the best parts of yourself literally makes you a better person. But if you are going to be courageous, an example for all those who are ready to step into their power, then you must be willing to show the world all of who you are. You must have the guts to throw off the chains of modesty and mediocrity in order to be the light that the world needs.

The only thing stopping you from being your whole authentic self is fear. Your fear tells you that you can't fulfill your dreams. Your fear tells you not to take risks. Your fear stops you from enjoying your richest treasures. Your fear keeps you living as the self that you've known rather than letting you expand to express the full spectrum of your magnificence. Your fear keeps you numb, blocking you from the exuberance and excitement of life. Anxious and fearful, you inevitably create situations in your life to prove to yourself that your self-imposed limitations are the truth. To overcome your fear, you have to face it and replace it with love.

Charlene came to the Shadow Process Retreat as the kind of person you would just walk by without knowing she was there, invisible. With her shoulders drooping, her head hanging, eyebrows that looked like they had never been tweezed, and a faint mustache on her upper lip, she told us that she was the associate vice president of a large investment firm. She had recently heard that she was about to be passed over for a promotion. A friend had let it slip that the frontrunner for the position was someone much less qualified and with far less seniority than Charlene had. When Charlene pushed her friend for an explanation of why the management team would consider such a candidate, her friend admitted, "Well, she's twenty years younger and more camera friendly than you are, and this position would be the face of the company."

Charlene was heartbroken, because she had given so much to the firm. She had stayed late, taken on extra projects, worked on weekends, and said yes to everything in anticipation of this advancement—one that would secure her financial independence for the rest of her life. She came into the workshop fully defeated and simply wanting to make peace with the fact that she was going to lose the promotion. Instead, I suggested that she pull herself up off the floor of failure. I urged her to fight for the position instead of succumbing to a future that was unacceptable to her.

I asked Charlene whether she felt that the way she looked and dressed was appropriate for such a senior position at her company. She angrily told me how horrible it was that she worked for a company, and lived in a world, that was so superficial and shallow. She argued that it shouldn't matter whether she looked like a rhinoceros with a pig's nose as long as she got the job done. She did her job and did it well. But as Charlene continued to vent, she began to experience the sadness underneath her anger. She could see that she showed up to work looking the way she did because it never occurred to her that it mattered. I asked her why she believed it didn't matter in such a high-level job, and she told me that to compete in a man's world she had to be taken seriously and not thought of as a woman. But, of course, there was much more to the story. Underneath that belief, she discovered that she didn't really care about herself. That's why she put her whole life into her work in the first place.

Then we started having fun. I asked her what she would do if she was going to have her looks not be an issue but, in fact, be an inspiration to the management team. How would she show up to her interview in eleven days if she were being an executive warrior, one who was courageous enough to seize what she deserved and take what was rightfully hers? We made a list. She would get her hair cut and colored at the best salon in Chicago. She would have a facial and have her eyebrows, her lips, and even the parts that you can't see waxed. She would call her best friend, who had impeccable taste, and have her find her a new style that was younger, more refreshing, and, in her words, "sexier." I suggested that she find a lace bra and underwear, something that made her feel really good. She would hire a trainer to work out with an hour a day just to help her feel like she was getting strong and toned. She would write out her case for why she was going to have this promotion, why she deserved it, and why nobody was going to take it away from her. She would practice her talk and have three friends hate it and argue with her about why she couldn't have the job and why somebody younger and better looking deserved it. They would stay with it until the argument held no power over her. It was imperative that she not get upset or hooked by anything the management team might say to her.

She had to become her own source of approval, and she had to believe in herself 100 percent. I told her how essential it was to start to reprogram any negative thoughts or fears into positive, affirmative acts of self-love. To do this, she would have to make a list every night of all the self-loving words she said to herself and all the self-loving things she did for herself that day. As soon as she got back to work, she would need to begin taking whatever steps she could before the big day. Charlene was now excited and turned on about the possibility of blowing all their minds, because now she was standing firmly in her courageous warrior. In my bones, I knew she would prevail.

A few months later, Charlene sent me a clipping from one of the financial magazines announcing her appointment as senior vice president of her firm.

Ralph Waldo Emerson once wrote, "Who you are speaks so loud I can't hear what you're saying." To feel like a confident and courageous warrior, you must look the part. You must take care of yourself as a precious, priceless messenger. You must reflect the value and esteem in which you hold yourself. It is time to take back your power—not for the approval of others, but for how you will feel inside. Self-love is the warrior's code and the fuel you will need to ride into your future with courage and confidence. There is nothing more beautiful than a warrior woman standing in her power, courage, and confidence. From this place of strength, she is capable of loving the world in a way that transforms pain into promise . . . and hell into heaven.

You may think that if you take the actions or if you say the words, you have done enough. You may think that you don't need to take responsibility for embodying the message you are sending. But if you think you can just say things without truly owning and embracing that which you already are, you are just putting ice cream on top of poop. If you aren't fully rooted in authenticity, one person can say something that in an instant can diminish your confidence. You are always communicating something about who you are and your belief in your own value. If you do not find the courage to embody your message on every level of your being, you will not reach the hearts that are waiting to be touched by you.

Everyone has different positive qualities that they have difficulty embracing and that they believe they don't actually possess.

I could argue this for the next thirty pages, but you'll just have to trust me. There is nothing you can see or desire in the outer world—no quality, characteristic, or trait—that you are not. I asked a group of my students to make a list of the positive qualities that they disowned—the ones that made them squirm, blush, or cringe when they imagined saying them out loud. Then I asked them to write love letters to themselves. I told them that the letters had to include at least five admissions of greatness that made them blush. It was amazing to me to observe how embarrassed they were just to write these things down, let alone say them out loud.

My Dearest, Sweet Isabella,

You are the light of my life. You astound me with your wisdom and insight. You are one of the most caring, compassionate, honest, trustworthy, loyal, loving, generous people I know. Your love is overflowing. And even though you have not always been on your best behavior, I forgive you and love you deeply. Anyone who meets you is fortunate to know you because of who you are. I cherish and value your divine presence.

With all my heart and love,
Isabella

Dear Emily,

I am in absolute awe at your deep dedication and infinite caring to help people live happier and healthier lives. I am amazed at the time and energy you devote to being the best you can be—you are unrelenting

*and unstoppable. Your deep intelligence, your clear insights into what
really matters, and your infinite trust in the goodness of people make
you the brightest star. You are living proof that nothing is impossible.
Your fear has hurt people, but the courage you've shown and the amends
you've made have helped you become a better woman. I am amazed
at your gumption, your bravery, and your intelligence. I love your
unselfishness. You are fearless and determined, a wondrous woman
warrior!*

With the deepest admiration and awe,

Emily

Dear Leah,

*How do I love thee? Let me count the ways. You are loving and kind,
funny and original, passionate and courageous, creative and insightful,
devoted and inspiring. You are a warrior woman—powerful, fiery, and
ready to take on the world. You are an amazing woman and my best
friend. I love you.*

Love,

Leah

Dear Alison,

*You are such a huge gift to the world, and I love how deeply you
love. You are magnificent in everything you do. All the ways you allow
your heart to shine make me smile from the inside out. You light up the
room with your beautiful presence, and those blue eyes are so rich that
everybody you meet feels your loving soul. You are so delightful and
sweet and nourishing. You are a breath of fresh air. Even the way you
speak is beautiful. Your humor is so funny that you crack me up. I just*

love how you share yourself in all of the ways you do. I cherish you
now and forever.

Love you,
Alison

When they read their love letters out loud, the whole vibration of the room changed. People's eyes were shimmering with inner strength and excitement, and they were ready now to take on and embrace their powerful, positive qualities. We set the students up in groups of four, with three people on one side and one person facing them in what we called the "Love Seat." The process began with the person in the Love Seat looking at the list she had made of the positive qualities she was disowning. Then, looking into the eyes of the people across from her, the person in the Love Seat said out loud, "I am _____."

I am lovable.
I am courageous.
I am confident.
I am powerful.
I am brilliant.
I am competent.
I am wise.
I am extraordinary.
I am unstoppable.

She powerfully proclaimed each positive quality, such as "I am unstoppable." And her three other group members repeated to her in unison, "You are unstoppable." The person in the Love Seat said it over and over and heard it reflected back to her until something shifted inside so that she was open to fully embracing this quality. It worked like magic. It was easy to see that when some people began, they didn't believe what they were saying. They had to breathe through their fear, their objections, and sometimes their revulsion. Some barely spoke the words, only whispering at first. Others cried because of how inadequate they felt. Still others shook their heads as they spoke. But always, each time, the person in the Love Seat broke through her resistance to the other side. It turned into a full-on celebration of love. By the end of their time in the Love Seat, many of them were standing on their chairs shouting . . .

I am loving!
I am confident!
I can do anything!
I am worthy!
I am fearless!
I am a superstar!

It was like popping the cork on a champagne bottle of inner possibility. The glee and joy were palpable. I was standing in the presence of the transformation that is possible for every person on the planet.

There is a warrior that exists inside you. It is there, but it has been ignored, repressed, and not allowed to come to fruition. The way to allow that warrior to have a voice is to become unrecognizable to yourself, to move outside your comfort zone, to let go of whatever you are holding on to, to release the self-image that you've kept trying to live up to over and over and over again. When you hold on to that image, which is probably an image from your past, the new version of yourself can never come out. There is a part of you—a courageous warrior—waiting to come to life.

If you've done the work in this book, you've stepped up already. You've done things you didn't want to do or things you didn't think you were capable of. You took risks. And if you continue in this way and allow yourself to be unrecognizable, you will do amazing things without even thinking about it.

As I was training a group of my coaches, I challenged them to take on being unrecognizable in some area of their lives—not one they figured out in their minds, but rather an area they felt pulled to by their heart or guided to by the Divine.

At my urging, when she realized that she was wearing the same bra she wore five years earlier, before her divorce, Evelyn went to Victoria's Secret for her very first bra fitting ever. Even though she'd lost fifty pounds, she was still scared of drawing attention to her body. But the thrill and the excitement of taking a risk so far outside her comfort zone quieted her fear. Although she didn't get the hot-pink lace bra that I suggested, Evelyn promised me that by the time this book came out she would have three bras in sexy, hot colors.

Molly grew up with a learning disability that had caused her great shame, embarrassment, and humiliation over the years. Feeling different, broken, and defective, she beat herself up for not processing information like everyone else. And although she had been coached by me for years to see her brain as highly creative and bearing its own unique gifts, she was afraid to give up her story, which had become a crutch that she used to keep herself from becoming a fantastic woman. To become unrecognizable to herself, Molly found a picture of a brain and drew rainbow colors all over it, each one representing her unique gifts and talents. Then she realized that helping others to be free of shame about the way they're "wired" would provide a whole new level of freedom for her, too. So she went to a school for developmentally disabled children and gave a talk to them on seeing their challenges as gifts from God.

Raisa, who spent hours listening to everybody else's drama and working on everyone's issues but her own, decided to give up being a caretaker and people pleaser. When one of her dear friends called and went on for over twenty minutes about different people (including friends of hers Raisa didn't even know), Raisa was finally able to speak up and say, "I'm sorry. I'm not really interested in your friend's story. I need to go now because I'm working on my own project." Setting a boundary, especially in the face of her fear that her friend would be mad at her, was totally foreign to Raisa. She hung up the phone and danced with glee. She could finally speak her truth.

Aubrey always saw herself as uneducated and unworthy because she had dropped out of college ten credits shy of her bachelor's degree. The shame she carried with her haunted her until she decided to finally handle it once and for all. To be unrecognizable to herself, Aubrey applied for admission to a local college, started taking classes, and is now working toward the completion of her four-year degree—something she had ignored and neglected for over thirty years.

After watching her father work like a dog at an insurance company for twenty years only to keel over from a heart attack at fifty-three, Bree vowed that she would never work for someone else and would always be self-employed. Being an entrepreneur meant survival to Bree. Even when her finances began to suffer, she ignored the nudges from the Divine to get a job. When she took on the challenge of being unrecognizable to herself, Bree found the courage and confidence to apply for an administrative position at a local technology firm, and now she shows up for work every day promptly at 9:00 A.M.

You, too, have the power to be unrecognizable to yourself and inspiring to all those around you. Just imagine what will be possible for you—who you can continue to become—when you step out of fear and step into the extraordinary beingness of the courageous warrior, a warrior of strength, power, love, and deep trust, a warrior in partnership with the Divine.

What does your warrior of love look like? Allow yourself to see an image, one that you will never forget, one you can call up morning, noon, and night, an image that brings a smile to your face, light to your eyes, and excitement to every miraculous cell vibrating throughout your body. Live in the knowledge that you are a gift to the world. Let yourself feel your heart wide open, knowing now that you hold the magic, whether it's a wand, a staff, the reins of your horse, or some other symbol that represents the authority you have claimed in the living of your life. See the image stamped permanently into your consciousness, and breathe in the words "I am a warrior for love."

I am a powerful warrior.
I embrace that I'm a warrior for love.
I allow myself to be one with the Divine.
I allow my heart to be open to all that there is.
I accept the magical powers that come with being a warrior of love.
I am a much-needed part of this divine imprint.
I love reinventing myself.
I love being unrecognizable to all those around me.
I give my heart and soul to God.
I am a warrior for love and I'm enough.
I am a warrior for love and I matter.
When I stand in being a warrior for love, all things come as they should.
I accept my badge, my duty, and my gift of being a warrior for love.
I will remember every day that I'm a warrior for love.
I can see myself as a warrior for love.
I am a warrior for love.

Repeat these words until you feel the presence, the beingness, and the beauty of your inner warrior in every bone, every fiber, every inch of your consciousness. You are a warrior for love, part of a group of warriors who can't be beaten, who can't be pushed aside, who can't be defeated by fear. This group has come together in the name of love to serve, heal, and fully enjoy this world. And with you firmly at our side, we can continue the journey into divine courage and confidence.

And so we end where we began. As Helen Reddy tells us:

You can bend but never break me
'cause it only serves to make me
More determined to achieve my final goal
And I come back even stronger
Not a novice any longer
'cause you've deepened the conviction in my soul

I am woman, watch me grow
See me standing toe to toe
As I spread my lovin' arms across the land
[. . .]

[. . .]
I am strong (strong)
I am invincible (invincible)
I am woman

Yes you are.

THE SUPREME BEAUTY PROCESS

Savor this process over the next week or two. Take your time, have fun with it, and enjoy. Be sure to set a beautiful tone by turning off your cell phone, lighting a candle, and putting on some soft music. Create a space that evokes your imagination and emotion. Then, with the hand of a courageous warrior, pick up your pen and explore.

1. **Making yourself blush:** Make a list of the positive qualities that you actually possess but disown. These are attributes that you easily notice in other people but don't really

believe you have—qualities that make you blush or smile whenever someone acknowledges them in you. Use this list as a reference:

Loving

Generous

Brilliant

Visionary

Kind

Charismatic

Creative

Wise

Compassionate

Capable

Intelligent

Profound

Inspiring

2. **Dear Courageous Warrior for Love:** Write a love letter to yourself that includes at least five admissions of your greatness. Spritz the letter with a hint of your favorite perfume when you're done writing, as a symbol of sealing in the self-love.

3. **Making your divine beauty even more visible:** See what you can do this week to make yourself a powerful reflection of your highest self:

Go get your makeup done by a professional.

Do a bra fitting at Victoria's Secret.

Get a consultation to make sure you're wearing the best colors.

Get whitening solution for your teeth.

Get a manicure and pedicure.

Get your hair cut and styled.

*Do a consultation to make sure you have the hair color that best
complements your skin, eyes, and style.*

Or pamper yourself in some other way that feels outlandish.

4. **Reflections of courage and confidence:** Let yourself see
   what your inner courageous warrior looks like. Create an
   image of her that you can easily see several times a day
   in order to affirm and draw forward this profound power
   within you. Connect with this image at least once in the
   morning, once in the afternoon, and once at night.

5. **Turn up the music:** Create a soundtrack for this next
   extraordinary chapter in your life by making a playlist of
   songs. Choose songs that remind you of your strength,
   your power, your courage, and your confidence. Choose
   songs that turn on your self-love light! Visit debbieford
   .com/courage for suggestions.

6. **Your mantra of courage:** Allow yourself to discover your
   own unique power statement that you can use as a mantra
   to bask in the essence of the courageous warrior and stay
   connected to your warrior of love. Keep it to one short
   sentence, knowing that it will be a power source for you
   for years to come.

7. **Letting supreme beauty take you further than you ever imagined:** Take on the exciting challenge of being unrecognizable to yourself and those around you. Choose one area of your life to focus on, and then do something far outside your comfort zone related to that area, something you never believed you could or would do. Be bold.

Courage Activator

It's time to be divinely hot! Buy sexy lingerie or some other accessory that makes you feel hot but that you would never wear because you think it's too over-the-top sexy. Then wear it. (Unless, of course, you're already a harlot. Then find something that you would never wear and go for it.)

Confidence Builder

Go out in public looking like a complete mess and pretend that you're the most beautiful woman in the world. Allow your whole body to be radiantly alive and vibrating with divine confidence. Add in the challenge of imagining that you are naked when you go out. (Of course, you aren't.) Studies show that you walk with more poise, have better posture, hold your stomach in, stand taller, and are overall more aware of your body when you imagine this. You're going to have a fabulous time doing this, I promise! The next day, go full-out beauty!

Courage and Confidence Bonus

Interview five different people to find out what they love about you, and write down the qualities they see in you.

The Courageous Warrior's Mandate

LOVE YOUR FEARS

It is time to love your fears more than anything you have ever loved before, knowing that these fears are where the door to enlightenment lives.

Thank your fears for always bringing you into the presence of the limited human mind.

Thank your fears for making you look at your life.

Thank your fears for reminding you that you have a small child inside that is in desperate need of your love and attention. Thank your soul for dispensing these fears to you to help you find your way back home to God—the energy of pure love, the energy that trumps fear.

Love your fears like you have loved no other part of you—bless them, honor them, and use them as the holy reminders that they are . . . reminding you always to come home to your whole self.

LOVE YOUR CONFIDENCE

It is time to see your confidence as the divine gift that will literally change your life forever.

Love your confidence for always showing you your true value, for owning up to your gifts, for speaking your truth even when you're scared, for wanting you to be more.

Thank your confidence for seeing a version of yourself beyond your own imagination and for inviting you into a holy dance of full self-expression.

Love your confidence for being a constant companion that always wants to come out from behind the curtain, even in the face of life's challenges.

Thank your confidence for rewarding you with the ability to reinterpret your life and to bring yourself powerful and empowering messages.

Love your confidence for allowing you to fake it until you make it.

LOVE YOUR COURAGE

It is time to love your courage like it is the most precious gold that you've ever been given.

Bless your courage. Thank it before you go to bed at night,

when you wake up in the morning, and every time you take one courageous step that fills your body with hope and strength.

Thank your courage for always being there even when you ignored it for years or pretended that you didn't have it.

Love your courage for holding the vision of you as a courageous warrior.

Thank your courage for allowing you to grow as big and strong as you've ever wanted to be and for giving you the strength to speak your truth and be your authentic self in ways you've never imagined.

Love your courage for always being there, whispering in your ear, "There is a higher choice to be made, and you have the strength to choose it."

LOVE YOURSELF

At the end of our journey, we come back to love. Ultimately, when we love all parts of ourselves, when we bless all of ourselves, when we honor all of our history and all of our insecurities, doubts, worries, and fears, we become the women that we always wanted to be. The greatest act of courage is to bring love where there is none. And the greatest act of love is to bring courage where there has been none and to bring confidence where we feel insecure. That is the love that we've all been waiting for. And that is the love that is you.

Now is time for you to take the Vow of the Courageous Warrior. Sign your name below. (If you don't want to write in your book, you can download the Vow at debbieford.com/courage.)

THE VOW OF THE COURAGEOUS WARRIOR

I, _____, will *no longer* be bound by the slavery of my fear.

I will *never* again give my power away to my insecurities, my doubts, or my resentments.

I will *stop* allowing my past to define who I am, and I will *stand* for my highest integrity.

I will *stop* being a people pleaser and will honor my authentic truth.

I will *stop* listening to the voice of my critical, fearful, arrogant, know-it-all self, and I *will* listen to the voice of my most courageous and confident self.

I will *break free* from the strangulating grip of my self-defeating behaviors and will each moment *choose* powerfully to make choices that leave me feeling strong, powerful, and ready to take on the world and move from fear to faith.

I take this vow *now* as a positive stand for my soul's highest expression and for every man, woman, and child on this planet today.

As I set myself free, I am freeing all those around me to be their courageous, confident, authentic selves.

And now, as I close my eyes, I ask all the powers that be to support me in living this vow each moment of each day.

So it is. And so it shall be.

_____

(Your signature)

Acknowledgments

I've always been inspired by the people who have helped me become who I am today. I could write a whole book on all those who support me, but I want you to know whether you're named or not, if you're in my life or in my programs, you have helped me embrace my most courageous self.

I'd like to personally thank:

My sister, Arielle Ford, and my brother-in-law, Brian Hilliard, for being my agents and always supporting me in making the highest choice.

My relentless, genius editor, Gideon Weil, and the entire fabulous team at HarperOne for being the best publisher I could have ever asked for.

Julie Stroud, my manager and executive assistant, who worked next to me all year to make this book possible, for all her brilliance and dedication. You inspire me.

The remarkable executives of the Ford Institute—Jeff Malone, Kelley Kosow, and Pernille Melsted—who every day allow my body of work to touch and transform lives through the programs the Institute delivers and the coaches it trains.

My courage supporters for all the love and care they send my way—Suzanne Todd; Rob Lee; Sherry Davis; Joyce Ostin; my brother, Mike Ford; his wife, Anne; and their wonderful family, Ashley, Eve, Sarah, Tyler, and Logan; Rachel Levy; Dr. Marin Xavier; Dr. Daniel Vicario; Michael Gerrish; Greg Zelonka; Mary Herndon; Amy McGrath; and Daniel Bressler.

The Integrative Coaches I trained who participated in my weekly Courage group for sharing their experiences, breakthroughs, and strength so I could share their stories with the world: Alisha Schwartz, Manfred Laube, Frances Fusco, Rochelle Schwartz, Angela Lambert, Cate LaBarre, Elizabeth ter Poorten, Eve Blaustein, Kalyn Block, Patricia Menaul, Raye Marske, Debora Bradley, Heather Passant, Debbie Moran, Desy Campbell, Karen Lanser, Marisa Harris, Mary Cunningham, Pia Christensen, Julie Brady, Patrice McKinley, Bette Schubert, Dwight Brown, Anne Porter, Sue Goodwin, Jean Lin, Lorraine Brock, Bonnie Lundrigan, Martina Caviezel, Tessa Brock, Claire Rall, Danielle Eidson, Lulu Mahaini, Christy Lee, Gitte Andersen, Connie Viveros, Katie Carlone, and Stacie Schmidt.

My dear friends Cynthia Kersey of the Unstoppable Foundation and Marjorie Morrison, author of *The Inside Battle*, for their inspired visions.

Nancy Levin, the author of *Writing for My Life: Reclaiming the Lost Pieces of Me*, for her words and poetry that so inspire me.

The exceptional Wayne Dyer for his inspiration and support and for being an extraordinary example of courage to us all.

Reid Tracy, Margarete Nielsen, and the sensational team at Hay House for giving me an incredible platform from which to get my work out in the world.

Geeta Singh and Talent Exchange for courageously booking me to lead seminars and speak around the world.

Scott Blum, Madisyn Taylor, and the DailyOM for providing a great home for the Overcoming Fear online course.

Oprah Winfrey, Corny Koehl, Jill Barancik, Lisa Weiss, and the OWN staff for giving me the opportunity to take a courageous leap out of denial and into authentic and vulnerable freedom.

My good friend Cheryl Richardson for affirming me into the courageous woman I am today.

My incredible mother, Sheila Fuerst, whose courage has been an inspiration to me always.

My amazing son, Beau, whose courage always inspires me to take another risk.

About the Author

Debbie Ford is a *New York Times* bestselling author of nine books and an internationally acclaimed teacher, speaker, transformational coach, filmmaker, and expert in the field of personal transformation. She has guided tens of thousands of extraordinary people to learn to love, trust, and embrace all of who they are. Debbie is a pioneering force in incorporating the study and integration of the human shadow into modern psychological and spiritual practices. She is the executive producer of *The Shadow Effect* movie, an emotionally gripping, visually compelling transformational documentary featuring Deepak Chopra, Marianne Williamson, and other provocative thinkers and beloved teachers.

Debbie is the founder of the Ford Institute for Transformational Training, the renowned personal and professional training organization that offers emotional and spiritual education based on her body of work to individuals and organizations around the world. She is also the creator and leader of the Shadow Process Retreat.

Connect with Debbie on Facebook at www.facebook.com/DebbieFordFanPage, on Twitter at www.twitter.com/Debbie_Ford, or on www.hayhouseradio.com.

If you want to continue to cultivate your courage and confidence, step out of your fear and into your greatness, and manifest greater love, abundance, health, and happiness, join Debbie, her staff, and her community of Integrative Coaches for life-changing workshops, online courses, trainings, and private coaching, or, as a first step, take the online course Overcoming Fear.

To learn more, visit
www.DebbieFord.com
www.TheFordInstitute.com